DISPLAYING THE WISDOM OF GOD

"To bring to light for everyone what is the plan of the mystery hidden for ages in God who created all things, so that through the church the manifold wisdom of God might now be made known." Ephesians 3:9,10

A Devotional Commentary on Paul's Letter to the Ephesians

DANIEL ESAU

WESTBOW
PRESS
A DIVISION OF THOMAS NELSON

ISBN: 978-1-4497-3770-2 (sc)

Library of Congress Control Number: 2012900959

WestBow Press books may be ordered through booksellers or by contacting:

WestBow Press
A Division of Thomas Nelson
1663 Liberty Drive
Bloomington, IN 47403
www.westbowpress.com
1-(866) 928-1240

Printed in the United States of America

WestBow Press rev. date: 3/29/2012

CONTENTS

WHY AND HOW

If you were to ask me why, at the ripe old age of 85, I would undertake to write a book I could give you a lot of reasons. I suppose first of all, if I am going to do it I better get started. Another reason is that some years ago I began to have a voice problem which put an end to my teaching. But, fortunately, I can still write and, more importantly, pound keys. A third and probably the least important but most motivational reason is that I have a lazy streak and I need an incentive to keep me in THE BOOK. My meditations in this wonderful work of Paul during the writing of this book have removed a great deal of boredom from swimming and lying awake at night. The writing of this commentary has been of immeasurable personal value to me. If anyone else should find some value in it that would be icing on the brownie (cake really needs icing, brownies not necessarily).

There have been so many involved in my writing this book that it is difficult to single out any one individual. The many teachers in several institutions, pastors, past and present, ministry associates and personal friends have all had a part it shaping my theology and, more importantly, my life. I especially appreciate those who have encouraged me in this endeavor. My special thanks to daughter Valerie (whose writing skills surpass mine), my good friend Bob Poland, church secretary Susan Hollins. My special thanks to Susan for assisting with grammar and corrections and to grandson Matthew Gibson for technical and artistic assistance.

My thanks also to Hewlett-Packard and Microsoft who were of immeasurable help (am a little irritated with them for not being available when I wrote my Master's thesis). I hope they enjoyed the many hours I spent in their company.

I should also inform you, before you begin reading, that my mind tends to work in summary form. This commentary records the results of my meditations but does not take you down the path of how I arrived at these results. I often chafe at preachers who seem to belabor a point. After a brief explanation and a concise illustration my mind is saying "you have made your point, now let's get on with the sermon". And that is probably why I don't excel as a preacher. Perhaps I assume too much from my hearers and readers. At any rate, your own meditations will add value to this book. To assist you in this I have inserted many Scripture references for your further consideration.

FORWARD

There are many excellent critical and exegetical commentaries, old and new, on this extraordinary book of the NT Canon. This commentary does not really fit into that category. If you are looking for an explanation of some difficult passage, I suggest you consult other commentaries. You may find this commentary unsatisfying. If, on the other hand, you are concerned about enhancing your own spiritual journey you may find some help here. My concern is not only for the conduct of our individual lives, but how they contribute to the life of the Church. Because, as Paul points out in 3:10, God's purpose for the Church is that "the manifold wisdom of God might now be made known to the rulers, and authorities in the heavenly places" (and, if Paul were writing today, he would surely include all those on earth who are looking in), since she, the Church, is "a pillar and buttress of truth" (I Tim. 3:15). I am deeply concerned about the spiritual condition of the church which is a reflection of the spiritual state of her members.

Ephesians 3:10 is a key verse and, in my view, explains Paul's purpose for penning this letter. The Church, directly or indirectly, constantly comes into view in every section. And, obviously, the character of the Church is fashioned by the character of its members. Fortunately, in this case the strength of the church is not measured by its weakest link. But each member of the body either contributes to or detracts from the Church's display of God's wisdom. I am not sure that it could be possible to neither contribute nor detract. Therefore each member of the Church must understand his, or her, new position as it relates to the new life and the personal responsibility to contribute to the Church's display of the wisdom of God. It seems to me there is a woeful lack of understanding of this personal responsibility by too many members of the body of Christ.

In the first three chapters of this letter Paul tells us what we need to know to fulfill our responsibility, and in the last three he tells us what we need to do in response. We can summarize the epistle briefly; "a new position demand a new walk." Part I deals primarily with the "head" (intellect) and the last part with the "will" (our response), with some "heart" (emotion) scattered through-out. We need to keep in mind, however, that there is considerable "will" involved in Part I, and a good bit of "head" involved in Part II.

I would be hard pressed to place this work in a specific literary genre. It is primarily a commentary but interspersed with a little biography, confession, and, quite a little preaching for which I make no apology. It is largely the product of my personal meditations of Ephesians over quite a few years, and especially in the past eight months. While I have not made use of other commentaries in writing this book my theology has obviously been fashioned by their use as I have taught Ephesians several times in the past. My primary resource in the preparation of this book has been the *Theological Dictionary of the New Testament,* edited by Gerhard Kittel. It has been a great help in understanding Paul's vocabulary. My preparation also included a BA degree from Taylor University, 1951, and an MTh from Dallas Theological Seminary, 1969.

All Scriptural quotations are from the English Standard Version of the Bible. Where a book of the Bible is not mentioned the quotation is from Ephesians. Pronouns referring to God are capitalized unless they are quotations from the ESV.

Daniel Esau, November, 2011

INTRODUCTION: 1:1-3

Paul, as in most of his letters, introduces himself as an apostle. This lends authority to what is taught in this letter which involves truth that is crucial to the believer's walk and to the believers' contribution to fulfilling God's purpose for the church. The letter is addressed to "the saints" whom he assumes are also "faithful". The words "in Ephesus" are not found in all the extant copies of this letter. This may very well indicate that it was a cyclical letter meant to be read not only to the church in Ephesus but to other churches as well, which seems to add additional importance to this letter. The letter was certainly appropriate for every church during Paul's time as it is for our own churches today. Perhaps this was the letter to Laodicea mentioned in Col. 4:16.

"Grace to you and peace from God our Father and the Lord Jesus Christ" are words that are found at the beginning of every one of Paul's letters. But this was not some rote phrase that automatically appeared at the beginning of each letter. His mission was to introduce the message of peace to every person (especially gentiles) which can be obtained only by God's grace. Both "peace" and "grace" are essential elements in this epistle. In Paul's letters to Timothy and Titus he adds the word "mercy". (perhaps thinking of the special needs of "pastors".)

PART I

WHAT WE NEED TO KNOW

Chapters 1, 2 and 3

"That I may know him and the power of his resurrection and may share his sufferings, becoming like him in his death." Phil. 3:10

CHAPTER 1

Ephesians 1:3-23

GOD'S PURPOSE

"For we are his workmanship, created in Christ Jesus
for good works, which God prepared beforehand,
that we should walk in them." Ephesians 2:10.

The believer's relationship to God's purpose, (1:3-14).

This section of Paul's letter to the Ephesians is usually titled "Spiritual Blessings in Christ". And that is not inappropriate since Paul describes a cascade of blessings that accrue to "the saints and faithful in Christ Jesus". But these blessings are not an end in themselves. The bigger picture here is how they equip believers to play a crucial role in displaying God's wisdom. God has a purpose in investing spiritual blessings in His people. Paul makes that very clear in this passage. His purpose in election was "that we should be holy and blameless before Him" (vs. 4). That He had some specific goal in mind through the bestowal of these spiritual blessings is quite obvious. They were "according to the <u>purpose</u> of his will" (vs.5), and, "according to his <u>purpose</u>" (vs. 9). Paul further states that we were "predestined according to the <u>purpose</u> of him who works all things according to the <u>counsel of his will</u>" (vs.11). If the bestowal of His blessings was for a specific purpose, and we are the recipients of those blessings, we need to give some attention to how we fit into His plan.

The initial blessing, election, ours long before we appeared, calls attention to His eternal purpose. The second blessing listed, predestination, is evidence that God is accomplishing His purpose. God does not elect us and then leave us to our own devices. Predestination guarantees that God continues to be involved in our lives. As we "grow in the grace and knowledge of our Lord and Savior Jesus Christ" (2 Peter 3:18) we also grow in our ability to display God's wisdom to the world. This is the "breastplate of righteousness" of the Christian's armor explained in chapter six. Our predestination (verse 11) is "according to the purpose of Him who works all things according to the counsel of his will". He is working out His purpose in us. Included is also our adoption, literally "sonship". All the rights of the firstborn son accrue to us, including the inheritance that awaits us.

Other blessings include redemption - release on payment of a penalty. In using this word Paul certainly had in mind the first redemption of Israel out of Egypt. The Passover lamb looked forward to the Lamb of God and the payment of a price that would redeem His people from the bondage of sin. And being redeemed, having the penalty for our sin paid, we enjoy forgiveness. The burden of guilt has been lifted and we now have "peace with God" (Rom. 5:1). All of these flow from the "riches of His grace with which He lavished upon us in all wisdom and insight" (1: 7,8). And all this was included in His plan for us, "according to His purpose, which he set forth in Christ" (1:8). The spiritual blessings God lavishes on us contribute to His final purpose which is "to unite all things in Him, things in heaven and things on earth" (1:10) and thus display His manifold wisdom.

In this initial doctrinal section of this letter we see the work of the triune God. In verses 4 through 6 the work of the Father is explained. He chose us (election), continues to be involved in our lives (predestination) all in accordance with His eternal plan. In verses 7 through 12 we see the work of the Son. In Him we have redemption, forgiveness of our trespasses, have obtained an eternal inheritance and much more. The work of the Holy Spirit is briefly outlined in verses 13 and 14. Here Paul states that we "are sealed with the promised Holy Spirit". In the purchase of property an offer to purchase is accompanied by "key money" which is a guarantee that we are serious and will follow through with the purchase. This "promise" (key money) of the Holy Spirit is God's guarantee that if His offer of salvation is accepted He will, without exception, bless us further with our "inheritance". The work of the trinity in man's redemption might be summarized as follows: God the Father planned it, God the Son executed the Father's plan, and God the Holy Spirit applied it to the believer. We are "born of the Spirit" (John 3:8).

All the blessings listed above are included in God's promise to His "elect". And it is obvious that they are "spiritual" and not "material". The blessings promised to Israel were primarily physical and material. In our dispensation the promised "spiritual" blessings also often overflow into the physical and material but this is in addition to and not part of the promise.

It is also important to note that these blessings are in Christ. They are ours only because of our relationship to God's Son. We are blessed in Christ (vs. 3), chosen in Him (vs. 4), we have redemption in Him (vs. 7), are united to Him (vs. 10), our inheritance is in Him (vs. 11) and we are sealed in Him (vs., 13). In Romans chapter 5 Paul reminds us that we came into this world as a member of the family of Adam. We are inheritors of his sin and therefore were subject to death. But "as in Adam all die, so also in Christ shall all be made alive" (I Cor. 15:22). By natural birth we were identified with Adam, but by spiritual birth we are now identified with Christ. "Therefore if any one is in Christ, he is a new creation. The old has passed away; behold, the new has come" (II Cor. 5:17).

Notice also that these "spiritual" blessings which are ours "in" Christ are also "in the heavenlies". Being in Christ allows us to look into and participate in a sphere of existence we, in our unregenerate state, never knew existed. While we are still in the physical world we have also become citizens of another non-physical world (Phil. 3:20). As Paul wrote in chapter 2, God has "raised us up with Him (Christ) and seated us with Him in the heavenlies" (vs. 6). Paul gives us some insight into the "heavenlies" in his letter to the Corinthians. He encourages them - and us - in the face of hardships to "look not to the things that are seen but to the things that are unseen. For the things that are seen are transient, but the things that are unseen are eternal" (II Cor. 4:17,18). The spiritual blessings are not visible to the naked eye. They are experienced only by faith and are more real than if we could see them. Be advised that life "in the heavenlies" is not without conflict as we will see when we get to chapter 6.

Paul's Prayer in Response to the Above (1:15-23).

Even a slow reader can read verses 3 to 14 in about 2 minutes. But a life time of study would fail to bring the reader to a complete understanding of its majestic presentation of God's truth. Perhaps Paul himself, may not have totally comprehend what the Spirit of God had lead him to record for the edification of His church. Realizing the difficulty his readers' might encounter in coming to an understanding of these doctrines of grace drove him to his knees. As we consider the degradation of our culture and the spiritual ignorance of many believers, should we not also spend more time on our knees in prayer for understanding God's truth?

The phrase "for this reason" (dia touto) is used at least 10 times in Paul's epistles. Following this phrase Paul lists the (or a) consequence of what precedes. And his prayer at this point was a consequence of the importance of the information he had just recorded. His prayer also arose from what he had learned of his readers faith in the Lord Jesus and their love for fellow believers. Much of our prayer should be composed of what we know about our fellow believers and their special needs. In order to pray effectively we need to keep up with the needs of our fellow believers and the growth of the church around the world. It never ceases to amaze - and disappoint - me at the poor attendance when missionaries speak in our fellowship. If we paid as little attention to our financial investments as we do to our investments in our missionaries and their activities, we might be in serious financial trouble. The more information we have, the more effective are our prayers. How crucial today is Paul's plea to the Corinthians. "You must help us by prayer, so that many will give thanks on our behalf for the blessing granted us through the prayers of many" (II Cor. 1: 11).

Paul, understanding the enormity of the truth he has presented knew that it could not be assimilated without earnest prayer. And so he prays! And he appropriately begins with thanksgiving (I guess the acronym ACTS had not yet been coined). Thanksgiving was certainly not foreign to the Apostle. He began his Roman letter with "I thank my God through Jesus Christ for all of you". He was equally thankful to God for the Corinthians, Philippians, Colossians and Thessalonians. Only in his letter to the Galatians did he not mention his thanks for them. He was evidently so astonished by their misunderstanding of the Gospel that thanksgiving momentarily escaped him. Perhaps not entirely unlike my father-in-law's request as we were sitting down to a meal of left-overs. "Dan, you ask the blessing. I can't be very thankful for this." We will see when we get to chapter 5 that being thankful is also one of the evidences of the filling of the Spirit!

For a spirit of wisdom and revelation

The content of Paul's prayer was quite different from the usual list of "gimmies" that too often define our prayers. His prayer was addressed to "the Father of glory" (now he has gotten around to the "A" of ACTS - Adoration). He prays first of all that they might have a spirit of wisdom and revelation. Wisdom would seem to be the ability to apply truth, and revelation an understanding of the truth that needs to be applied. Revelation is truth revealed only by God and only the Spirit could "enlighten" the "eyes of your hearts" to comprehend it, and give us the ability to apply it.

To know the hope to which they were called

He then prayed that they would "know what is the hope to which he has called you." Hope is one of the three enduring qualities that accompany faith and love (I Cor. 13:13) and is the possession only of believers. Paul reminded them - and us - that before they became one in Christ they were "separated from Christ, alienated from the commonwealth of Israel and strangers to the covenant of promise, having no hope, and without God in the world (2:12). Hope is living in the understanding that all God's promises will be fulfilled. "In hope (Abraham) believed . . . . that he should become the father of many nations, as he had been told" (Rom. 4:18). It was this hope, accompanied by faith, that kept him focused on the path God had purposed for him. "For he was looking forward to the city that has foundations, whose designer and builder is God" (Heb. 11:10).

Is our vision of our ultimate goal, and the path God has chosen for us to get there, any less focused than was Abraham's? Are we aware that at this very moment God is at work in us accomplishing His purpose for electing us (1:4)? Paul, commenting on the ministry of the New Covenant stated "since we have such a hope, we are very bold" (II Cor. 3:12). Is boldness a concept that comes to mind when we think of our witness? May God bring our desire to "know what is the hope to which He has called us" into sharper focus.

To know the riches of their inheritance

His next request is that they would know "the riches of His glorious inheritance in the saints." He wrote earlier (1:11) that in Christ "we have obtained an inheritance". Inheritance does not depend on activity but on a relationship. We look forward to an inheritance only because we are in Christ. In Christ we were adopted into the family of God. We have become children, "and if children, then heirs -- heirs of God and fellow heirs with Christ" (Rom. 8:17). To this last statement he adds "provided we suffer with Him in order that we may also be glorified with Him." This declaration of Paul deals with the evidence of our position as children, not as works that need to be performed to obtain an inheritance.

When my father died our financial inheritance was in the form of medical bills. Fortunately there were enough heirs (7) so the burden was light. But he left us something far better than things. He left us an example of a life totally committed to his Father, resulting in 7 children who follow his Lord. Fathers, what does your spiritual estate look like? In view of the "glorious inheritance" that we look forward to, let's make sure that our estate contains more than "things"!

To know the greatness of His power

To be actively and fruitfully involved in pursuing God's purpose for us we also must understand "the immeasurable greatness of His power" (1:19a) which is available to us who believe. This power was most powerfully displayed when He raised Jesus from the dead. The last enemy to be destroyed was death which was "according to the working of His great might" (1:19b). It must necessarily have been great because when he raised Christ all the rest of us who are in Christ were raised with Him.

Jesus' final words to His disciples were "But you will receive **power** when the Holy Spirit has come upon you" (Acts 1:8). And the events recorded in the rest of the book of Acts are a tremendous display of the power of God. And this power was exercised by men who by earthly standards were "uneducated, common men" (Acts 4:12). And Paul identified with these men. He was highly educated but had no confidence in his education. To the Corinthians he stated, I "did not come to you with lofty speech or wisdom. For I decided to know nothing among you except Jesus Christ and Him crucified." He further stated "I was with you in weakness and in fear" (I Cor. 2:1-3). After he had pleaded with God three times to remove his "thorn" (poor eyesight?) God's response was, "My grace is sufficient for you, for my **power** is made perfect in <u>weakness</u>" (II Cor. 12:9).

If God's power is perfected in weakness, then we are all eminently qualified to fulfill the purpose God has for each one of us. We have absolutely no excuse for being mere observers when others are engaged in kingdom activity. God has gifted every believer to be a useful part of His work force. Are we all contributing to the display of God's wisdom to the world? God intends for His glory to be displayed and the best way to do that is for lives to be changed by the Gospel. It is our responsibility to be faithful witnesses to the Gospel but our responsibility ends there. The response depends on God who makes the Gospel "the **power** of God for salvation to everyone who believes" (Rom. 1:16).

God's power was not exhausted when he raised Jesus from the dead. He elevated him to a seat at his right hand - a place of power and authority. He is above the "heavenlies", directing the affairs of this world. He is above the "heavenlies" described in chapter 6 and verse 12 where His power is available in our struggle "against the rulers, against the authorities, against the cosmic powers over the present darkness, against the spiritual forces of evil in the heavenly places (heavenlies)".

Paul further reminds us that God "put all things under his feet" (1:22), another picture of Jesus' authority over all the earth. Not only is He the creator of all things but "in him all things hold together" (Col. 1:17). And the climax of Paul's prayer for their understanding of the truth he has just presented is that God "gave Him as head over all things to the church." He adds, "which is His body, the fullness of Him who fills all in all." We need only to ask that His power become available to us so we will adequately display his manifold wisdom to an ignorant world.

Christ as Head of the Church

In May 1963 an article by A. W. Tozer appeared in the Alliance Witness titled "The Waning Authority of Christ in the Churches". He wrote "Jesus Christ has today almost no authority at all among the groups that call themselves by His name". And the situation of the past half century has certainly not improved. The mainline denominations in their discussions of subjects like ordination, sexual orientation etc., seek the input of every kind of "expert" but have no intention of considering what the head of the Church might have to say about them. Dr. Tozer is quick to point out that the evangelical Church is not without guilt. Too often we make our decisions and then ask God to bless what we have decided without seeking His input. Too often how we "feel" about something is the deciding factor. Emotion is a wonderful companion but a terrible master. Our discussions about contemporary versus traditional "worship" have often produced more heat than light. We must allow the "Head" of the church to actually be the head. Do we depend upon Him to actually control our activity?

Then Paul adds, almost incidentally, that the church is Christ's body. The relationship of the church to its head could not be more intimate. That the body would operate on its own apart from the direction of the head is unthinkable. As a child, I was fascinated by the actions of a chicken after Dad had separated its head from its body. It expended a great amount of energy but accomplished nothing. Unfortunately, the same can be stated of the church. Actions not directed by the Head accomplish nothing.

If the church is defined as a "body" then its members also sustain an intimate relationship to one another. Paul deals with this relationship in his first epistle to the Corinthians (12:12-31). God has given members of the church spiritual gifts which they are to use in ministry to the body. No gift, no matter how important it may seem, is superior to any other. Each gift is not in competition with, but is complimentary to, other gifts and is essential to the building up of the body. Do you suppose that our gifts are as important to displaying God's wisdom as were Paul's?

CHAPTER 2

Ephesians 2:1-22

RECONCILIATION

"And through him to reconcile to himself all things,
whether on earth or in heaven,
making peace by the blood of his cross."
Colossians 1:20

Chapter two of Ephesians gives us an account of what took place between verses four and five of Chapter one. Verse four had informed us that we were chosen by God to salvation in eternity past. His purpose in choosing us was "that we should be holy and blameless before him" (1:4). Verses five and following give us an account of God's work in the lives of His elect to fulfill His purpose. The blessings are that those who were the first to hope in Christ, and, obviously all who followed, might be to the praise of His glory (1:12). In order to fulfill that function there must be a two-fold reconciliation.

Reconciliation with God (2:1-10)

But long after our election, after God's work of verse 1:4 and before His work of verse 1:5 and following, we were still dead "in the trespasses and sins" (2:1). We were still very dry bones like the ones God showed to Ezekiel lying in the valley. And like these bones that God caused to come together, and be clothed with sinew and flesh and skin, so in our physical birth God invested us with flesh and blood. But again like Ezekiel's bones, there was no life yet (Ezek. 37).

The Ephesians (and we) were still "dead in the trespasses and sins" (2:1). They were walking in their sins, "following the course of this world, following the prince of the power of the air, the spirit that is now at work in the sons of disobedience" (2:2). Paul recognized where they were because he had been there. He also had, with others, "once lived in the passions of our flesh carrying out the passions of our body and the mind" (Rom. 7:5). And they "were by nature children of wrath, like the rest of mankind" (2:3). This is where the Ephesians were before they became the recipients of God's blessings. And Paul seems to infer that this is the "normal" condition of mankind. This is where most of the inhabitants of this world live. Jesus reminded us that the road to destruction is wide and easy and thronged with travelers. "For the gate is narrow and the way is hard that leads to life, and those who find it are few" (Math. 7:14).

But God had other plans for these Ephesians (and others - past and present). And His actions now are based on mercy. This attribute of God is a staple of Scripture. The Hebrew word for mercy (chesed) is found more than 100 times in the Psalms - in every one of the 36 verses of Psalm 136. And this God, who is rich in mercy, chose to give life to those who were "dead in our trespasses" (2:5). As the breath from God brought Ezekiel's dry bones to life, even so, he "made us alive together with Christ . . . and raised us up with him and seated us with him in the heavenlies (2:6).

And all this was a result of "the immeasurable riches of his grace" (2:7). Dead men have no ability to contribute or even to choose. So God's work in our lives is totally based on grace. We could add nothing to it so we have absolutely no reason to boast. It is all of grace! And it comes to us through faith which is also a gift of God. "For by grace have you been saved through faith" (2:8).

Daniel Esau

There has been some discussion about what the gift refers to since the word is singular. But it obviously has reference to both. Grace and faith go together (like "love and marriage" and "horse and carriage" - remember Doris Day?) "Grace" like "love" is rather a nebulous concept when taken by itself. To fully understand it, it demands an object.

And the object of grace is God's treatment of us. His election and all the other blessings described in Chapter one are completely undeserved. Someone (don't remember who) once remarked that there was something about the story of Jacob and Esau he didn't understand. How could God "hate" Esau? Someone listening in said there was also something about the story he didn't understand. "I don't understand how God could love Jacob". There is no way to fathom the mind of God, who, because of His great mercy granted us repentance and faith. Faith is God's gift as the object of His grace. And we begin to understand Grace when we contemplate His treatment of us.

The final verse of this section ties this in to God's purpose for His children and places it firmly between verses four and five of Chapter one. His election of us guaranteed that the spiritual blessings enumerated would follow because "we are his workmanship, created in Christ Jesus for good works which God prepared beforehand that we should walk in them". This is our response to God's blessings.

Reconciliation to Unity in one Body (2:11-22)

After God made it difficult for people to communicate with one another at Babel (Gen. 11), men have become more and more alienated from each other. Today there are more than 170 countries and there are many groups within some countries. We seem to have a great deal of trouble getting along with each other. Unfortunately, we have carried that characteristic of fallen man into the church. Paul felt it was necessary to exhort believers in all the churches to be at peace with one another (Rom. 16:17, I Cor. 1:10, Gal. 3:28, Phil. 4:2, Col. 3:11, I Thes. 4:6).

14

Out of the various groups that had coalesced God chose one man who would be the recipient of His special blessing. God cut a covenant with Abraham (Gen. 15) promising to make a great nation from his offspring. As a result the nation of Israel was born and became a mighty force because of God's promise to Abraham. All other of the earth's families remained "alienated from the commonwealth of Israel" (2:12). Under the old covenant a relationship with God was dependant on becoming a part of Israel. A foreigner would have to undergo circumcision and submit to the dictates of the Mosaic law.

Now, under the new covenant everything has changed. You (we) Gentiles, once considered "The uncircumcised" (I Sam. 17:26), "having no hope and without God in the world" (2:12) "who were once far off have been brought near by the blood of Christ" (2:13). By His death he abolished "the law of commandments and ordinances" (2:15) thus breaking "the dividing wall of hostility" (2:14) between Jew and Gentile. With the doing away of the law of commandments and ordinances there was no longer a need to go through Israel for a relationship with God. "For he himself is our peace, and has made us both one (2:14) "and might reconcile us both to God in one body through the cross" (2:16). "So then you are no longer strangers and aliens, but you are fellow citizens with the saints and members of the household of God . . ." (2:19).

When Paul states that the Old Testament system was abolished he is not stating that it no longer has value. But as a system it has no longer value in reconciling men to God. Now we both, Jew and Gentile, "have access in one Spirit to the Father" (2:18). His purpose was to "create in himself one new man in place of the two. . ." (2:15). This "new man", made up of Jew and Gentile (includes every non-Jew) is the church, and has come into being through the <u>activity</u> of Jesus Christ. Those who were "far off" have been brought near by the <u>blood of Christ</u> (2:13). <u>He</u> broke down the dividing wall (vs. 14). <u>He</u> created one new man instead of two (2:15). <u>He</u> reconciled both to God in one body (2:16). through <u>Him</u> we both have access in one Spirit to the Father (2:18). Here he reiterates the importance of our relationship to the Father through the Son. To be a part of

His body and be the recipient of His blessings depends on our being in Him.

Several times in his writings the Apostle has used the human body to illustrate the operation of the church. The health of the body depends on the proper functioning of each part. And the proper functioning of the Church, the body of Christ, depends on each member using his gift(s) in ministering to that body. And so he reminds his readers that Christ is the head of the church which is His body, made up of those who are the recipients of God's blessings. Paul uses the body as an illustration of the church in some detail in I Cor. 12. For the church to function properly each member is responsible to contribute, just as all parts of the human body work together for its growth and preservation. Here in Ephesians 2 he compares the church to a building. Erecting a structure requires architects, excavators, masons, carpenters, plumbers, electricians, painters and more. Each one contributes his own expertise to provide a useful building, which is an appropriate picture of how the church functions.

The Greek word for building (oikodomeo) is an important word in the New Testament. It is used literally in the Gospels for erecting buildings. The wise man "built" his house upon the rock, etc. We might think of the word being used figuratively when Christ, after Peter's confession (Math. 16:16) said "on this rock I will build my church". But this "building" is just as literal, although in a different way. Paul used the word in this way in his letters and it is usually translated as "edify". Paul also wrote that love "builds up" (I Cor. 8:1), all things don't "build up" (10:23), the one who prophesies "builds up" and "therefore encourage and "build" one another up (I Thess. 5:11).

Erecting buildings is a satisfying occupation because it displays the fruit of our labor. I always enjoyed painting because it revealed some accomplishment, often removing unsightly stains from view and leaving beauty in its place. When we use our God given abilities there ought also to be visible results. Our evangelistic efforts (whether having the spiritual gift of evangelism, or just being faithful witnesses) should result is seeing lives changed and, in most instances, growth in the body. Exercising our teaching abilities ought to produce mature believers. Being faithful in prayer ought, among many other things, make the ministry of the missionaries we support more fruitful.

Paul reminded the Corinthians "do you not know that your body is a temple of the Holy Spirit" (I Cor. 6:19)? And in this last verse of Ephesians two he adds "In him you also are being built together into a dwelling place for God by the Spirit." Here the "church' again comes into full view. God is building His church and every member is responsible to contribute bricks to that building. Paul picks this up again in chapter four when he pens "from whom the whole body, joined and held together by every joint with which it is equipped, when each part is working properly, makes the body grow so that it builds itself up in love" (4:16).

CHAPTER 3

Ephesians 3:1-21

A MYSTERY REVEALED

*"To them God chose to make known how great
among the Gentiles are the riches of the glory
of this mystery. Which is Christ in you,
the hope of glory." Colossians 1:27*

When Paul in verse one of chapter three repeats the phrase he used in chapter one, "for this reason", you would expect another prayer to follow. But before his prayer begins he sees the need to present additional information to them. The phrase "for this reason" will appear again in verse 14 followed by the expected prayer.

This strongly suggests that what is recorded between the two "for this reason" phrases is parenthetical. This "stewardship of God's grace" (3:2) that had been given to him was (is) a concept so foreign to fallen human nature that it calls for additional explanation. He identifies himself here as a "prisoner for Christ Jesus on behalf of you Gentiles" (3:1). His purpose in identifying himself as a prisoner was probably to stress the importance of his ministry because it had cost him a great deal. It was not something he had sought, but it was thrust upon him by God. This "mystery" had come by divine revelation. "For I did not receive it from any man, nor was I taught it . ." (Gal. 1:12).

Paul had been well prepared to be the messenger of the mystery. As a Pharisee he was familiar with the Hebrew Scriptures. He had certainly at some time in his life read the Prophets including the prophecy of the New Covenant in Jeremiah 31. That God had a special plan for Paul was revealed to Ananias (Acts 9:15) who may well have passed this information on to Paul. And Paul, before he had the opportunity to be influenced by the other apostles, spent some time alone in Arabia. I imagine he spent a great deal of this time meditating on Old Testament Scripture, especially on prophecy, and, with additional inspired information from the Holy Spirit, solidified his theology.

Paul was not the only recipient of revelation. He stated that this new body of Jew and Gentile was "built on the foundation of the apostles and prophets" (2:20). And, this mystery "has now been revealed to his holy apostles and prophets by the Spirit" (3:5). But there seems to be something unique about his comprehension of the Gospel. He appears to have been one of the leaders at the Jerusalem Council (Acts 15, Gal. 2:11, f). Peter seems to recognize Paul's leadership when he writes of "the wisdom given him" (II Peter 3:15) and may, himself, not have totally understood Paul's teaching (II Peter 3:16).

Paul recognized his special stewardship and was amazed by it since he considered himself "the very least of all the saints" (3:8). His humility was also displayed in his first letter to Timothy (1:15) where he considered himself the foremost of sinners. If we haven't, at one time or another, considered ourselves the vilest of sinners, we haven't fully understood the righteousness of God or the depravity of man.

Paul identified this special stewardship as a "mystery". A mystery in Scripture refers to a truth that had been hidden but now has been revealed by God. By using this word he intimates that something has changed in God's dealing with man. How significant you consider this difference will depend on your theological assumptions (Admit it! We all have them!). Many who subscribe to Covenant Theology might consider this as a mere "bump in the road" in God's dealings with man. Gentile believers have in a sense been spliced into His people, Israel. The church was born in Eden, or with the call of Abraham. Those who are more friendly with dispensational views will consider the difference more significant. The church was born at Pentecost (Acts 2) and Israel continues to exist as a separate group. I have a feeling that when the dust finally settles (end of the age) we are all going to say, after being enlightened by eternal truth, "How could I have missed that".

But regardless of where we began, Paul leaves no doubt as to where we will end up. Gentiles are now fellow heirs with all who share Abraham's faith (Rom. 4:16). This relationship "was not made known to men in other generations" (3:5). God gave to Paul special insight into the make-up of this relationship. He referred to this as a "stewardship of God's grace" (3:2) of which he "was made a minister" (3:7). The substance of the mystery "is that the Gentiles are fellow heirs, members of the same body, and partakers of the promise in Christ Jesus through the gospel" (3:6). Writing to the Colossians he described the mystery as being "Christ in you, the hope of glory" (Col. 1:27).

God's purpose in all of this was "to bring to light for everyone (Jew and Gentile) what is the plan of the mystery hidden for ages in God who created all things" (3:9). That God had a purpose in all of His dealings with men, Paul mentioned three times in the initial section of this epistle (1:5, 9, 11). God's election, predestination and all that followed had a specific purpose. Paul now identifies that purpose that in this age "through the church the manifold wisdom of God might now be made known to the rulers and authorities in heavenly places" (3:10). And Paul adds "this was according to the eternal purpose that he has realized (brought to pass) in Christ Jesus our Lord." (vs. 11).

It seems to me that this eternal purpose of God has not received the attention it deserves. This did not originate with Paul. In Exodus

(9:16) God spoke to Moses "and your people" (vs. 15), "But for this purpose I have raised you up, to show you my power, so that my name may be proclaimed in all the earth." And this was a recurring theme in the Psalms. "Sing to the Lord, bless his name; tell of his salvation from day to day. Declare his glory among the nations, his marvelous works among all the peoples" (Psalm 96:2,3).

Back to "for this reason" and Prayer No. 2

In view of the revelation of the "mystery" and God's purpose for the church, "for this reason" Paul is again ready to "bow my knees before the Father". Paul is following his own exhortation to the Thessalonians to "pray without ceasing" (I Thess. 5:17). In his first prayer (1:15-23) he made four specific requests. He prayed that his readers might be given a spirit of wisdom and revelation: that they would know the hope to which they were called: would know the riches of their inheritance, and what is the greatness of His power toward believers. In this prayer of chapter three he picks up where he left off with his first prayer. He prays that they would be "strengthened with power through the Spirit in your inner being" (3:16). And further, "may have strength to comprehend with all the saints what is the breadth . . ." etc. (3:18).

It would require extra spiritual strength to understand the "mystery" Paul had decoded for them and even more to respond to the exhortation "to display the manifold (many faceted) wisdom of God". At this point it might be good to remind ourselves again that God's strength - that which is greatly needed - is perfected in our weakness.

"Every family in heaven and on earth" (3:15) probably has reference to all believers, those who have died and those living, both Jew and Gentile. Entry into this family is through the one whose "name is above every name" (Phil. 2:9). And it is fitting that this family should bear His name since it is only in His name that entry can be gained. "For there is no other name under heaven given among men by which we must be saved" (Acts 4:12). And Paul's prayer for their strengthening was on the basis of "the riches of his glory" (3:16) and not because of any personal merit they might have or would obtain. He reminded the Philippians of this when he assured them that "God will supply every need of yours according to his riches in glory in (through the mediation of) Christ Jesus" (Phil. 4: 19).

Paul prayed that they would be "strengthened with power through his Spirit . . So that Christ may dwell in your hearts through faith" (3:16, 17). In chapter one Paul had stressed the importance of and the privilege of being "in Christ". That is his normal way of illustrating our relationship with Jesus Christ. "There is therefore now no condemnation for those who are in Christ Jesus" (Rom. 8;1). "If anyone is in Christ he is a new creation" (II Cor. 5:17). To Timothy he writes of "the salvation that is in Christ Jesus. . ." (II Tim. 2:10). In Romans he also states that we were all baptized into Christ Jesus (Rom. 6:3). In this prayer he illustrates that same relationship by stating that Christ also is in us, "so that Christ may dwell in your hearts through faith" (3:17). He also uses this figure in his letter to the Colossians. He describes the "mystery" as being "Christ in you" (Col. 1:27).

Knowing that we are in Christ gives us a sense of security. It is a place of protection and comfort. The additional truth that He is in us reminds us that His resources are available to us. He will fight our battles for us. "He who is in you is greater than he who is in the world" (I John 4:4). And it is God's gift of faith (2:8. 3:17) that makes us conscious of His presence and His ability to turn our weakness into strength.

He also prays that they would be "grounded" and "rooted" in love. One of these verbs would probably have been sufficient. But his superfluity revealed the importance he placed on this quality. He doesn't differentiate between God's love for us and our love for Him and he probably has both in view. Paul had written the Galatians "For the whole law is fulfilled in one word: you shall love your neighbor as yourself" (Gal. 5:14). His thoughts were undoubtedly going back to Jesus' words to His disciples. "You shall love the Lord your God with all your heart and with all your soul and with all your mind. This is the great and first commandment. And a second is like it: you shall love your neighbor as yourself" (Mk. 12:30,31). It's logical to think of these two commandments as one. Apart from God's love for us it would be impossible to love our neighbors. Love is a characteristic that will live forever. Paul, writing to the Corinthians, wrote of the three abiding qualities; faith, hope, and love, "but the greatest of these is love" (I Cor. 13:13). Faith will one day become sight, our hope will one day be realized, but love will never become extinct.

We usually expect the doxology to come at the end of a sermon or some kind of message. But Paul often exceeds our expectations and inserts doxologies in various places as he is no doubt overwhelmed by the information revealed to him. One such doxology appears in Rom. 11:33. Having just written about God's gracious dealing with Jew and Gentile he breaks into praise to God. "Oh the depth of the riches and wisdom and knowledge of God! How unsearchable are his judgments and how inscrutable his ways." (I was once informed that the goal of theology was to unscrew the inscrutable.) And after informing the Ephesians of all that God has done for them and how he expects them to respond he again breaks out into a doxology: "to him who is able to do far more abundantly than all that we ask or think" (3:20,21). When we voice our appeals to God we need to be convinced that He will respond (positively or negatively). Our minds need to be strengthened to understand God's will and how we must respond to it. Our earnest desire should be to think God's thoughts after Him.

PART II

WHAT WE NEED TO DO

Chapters 4,5 and 6

*"For we are his workmanship, created in Christ
Jesus for good works, which God prepared beforehand,
that we should walk in them." Ephesians 2:10*

CHAPTER 4

Ephesians 4:1-16

EQUIPPING

"And he gave the apostles, the prophets,
the evangelists, the pastors and teachers,
to equip the saints for the work of ministry,
for building up the body of Christ."
Ephesians 4:11,12

It was approaching 12 noon and a young boy who had been sitting in a pew beside his father asked, as the pastor finished his closing prayer, "is it done yet?" Dad's answer revealed some spiritual insight as he replied, "No, son, the sermon is over but now we have to "live it". In Part I of Ephesians Paul has laid out in some detail the new position believers now enjoy. And, in this new position, they have a responsibility to display the manifold wisdom of God in a world, if not controlled by, at least heavily influenced by Satan and his minions. If Part I is the sermon, Part II is the application. Now we have to "live it!", and in Part II Paul outlines God's plan to equip believers to carry out His plan.

Unity

Initial Appeal to a Worthy Walk

This new entity, the Church, is made up of many individuals and so the first order of business is to get them united - working together for a common purpose. Paul presents himself again as a prisoner (see 3:1) which may have been an added incentive for them to respond positively to his appeals. His first appeal is for them "to walk in a manner worthy of the calling to which you have been called" (4:1). Paul often used the word "walk" to describe how one conducted his life. In chapter two referring to their former life he wrote "among whom you once walked". In the ESV the word walk is translated as "lived". God's wisdom is displayed by those who "walk not according to the flesh but according to the Spirit" (Rom. 8:4). A worthy walk can only be produced by God's Spirit working in us. If Part I of this letter describes the new position believers are in, then Part II describes how they are to "walk" in view of their new position.

The Foundational Qualities.

Humility

Paul lists 3 qualities that are essential to laying a groundwork for walking in a worthy manner and building unity. He begins with the area of our life that we may have the most difficulty with: humility. In the first garden Satan told Eve that eating the fruit God had forbidden them to eat would make her wise. He stirred the pride in her heart that she, Adam and all their progeny, would struggle with up to the present time. We are still slow to understand that pride leads to destruction (Prov. 16:18). If we are to display God's wisdom we will do well to follow Peter's advice; "Clothe yourselves, all of you, with humility toward one another, for God opposes the proud but gives grace to the humble" (I Pet. 5:5). This exhortation is echoed by James (Jas. 4:6). It seems like those of us who struggle hardest with pride have the least to be proud of.

Gentleness

Gentleness is humility in action in our relationships with one another. Paul informs us that Jesus demonstrated this quality in His life. He described Jesus as meek and gentle (II Cor. 10:1). Gentleness is the opposite of harshness. Paul gave the Corinthians the option of his coming to them with a rod "or with love in a spirit of gentleness" (I Cor. 4:21). Timothy was instructed to pursue this quality (I Tim. 6:11) so, among other things, he could correct "his opponents with gentleness" (II Tim. 2:25). Titus was instructed to remind his congregation "to be gentle and to show perfect courtesy toward all people" (Tit. 3:2). The word "gentlemen" is not used often these days, perhaps for good reason.

Patience

The word for patience is literally "long on anger" (makrothumia). Patience is a discipline that endures difficulties without becoming angry or frustrated. Timothy was informed that God had used Paul "to display his perfect patience as an example of those who were to believe" (I Tim. 1:16). Paul would suffer greatly at the hands of many without any thought of reprisal. James lists the prophets as examples of patience and also adds Job to that list (James 5:10,11). In his intense suffering he would say "The Lord gave and the Lord has taken away, blessed be the name of the Lord" (Job 1:21). It takes this kind of patience to bear "with one another in love" (4:2) and to be "eager to maintain the unity of the Spirit in the bond of peace" (4:3, and also Col. 3:12,13).

We need to earnestly cultivate humility, gentleness (word - prautetos - is also translated as meekness in various places) and patience if we are to minister to one another in the body of Christ. As in the human family, in the church family there are children in various stages of maturity. There are infants - new believers - who need a great deal of attention (including activities not unlike changing diapers), while there are mature believers who require little attention. In between there are those who need different amounts of attention and all need continuous comfort and encouragement. We become more able to minister to one another as we grow in humility, gentleness and patience.

In a lecture to Dallas Seminary students Dr. J. Vernon McGee suggested that all believers should wear a sign stating "This is not the best the grace of God can do!". When he arrived the next morning to continue his lectures someone had hung a sign on his lectern "This is not the best the grace of God can do!". All believers, including us octogenarians, continue to be involved in the maturing process. No one, not even the Apostle Paul has yet arrived at complete maturity (Phil.3:15). If the process is to continue we need to be "eager (the sound of the Greek word "spoudazomai" contributes to the meaning of this word) to maintain the unity of the Spirit . . ." (4:3). And without the continuing exercise of humility, gentleness and patience it will never happen. May God help us to cultivate these desperately needed characteristics.

The Basis for Unity.

One Body

It is important to remember that Paul's instruction is to "maintain" unity, not establish it. Men have attempted to build organizations that encompass all believers (WCC for example) but have failed. The unity has already been established by the Holy Spirit, if we could only comprehend it. In the Spirit founded unity we are reminded that there is only one body. It seems to be part of fallen human nature to divide into groups. That may have begun when God interrupted the construction of the tower of Babel by making communication impossible. Paul experienced this disruption of unity at Corinth where the members began to line up behind different leaders: Paul, Apollas, Cephas (I Cor. 1:10-17). Today's televangelists take on rock star status and develop huge groups of followers. In this one body we have only one leader. It is our Lord Jesus Christ whom God placed as head of the churh "which is his body, the fullness of him who fills all in all" (1:22,23). If we rally around Him the unity of the body will be maintained.

b. One Spirit

This <u>one body</u> is activated and sustained by <u>one Spirit</u>. We enter the body as we are born by the Spirit (John 3). For "anyone who does not have the Spirit of Christ does not belong to him" (Rom. 8:9), and "for in one Spirit we were all baptized into one body . . ." (I Cor. 12:13). But that is not the end of the Spirit's ministry. The Spirit is the ultimate educator (John 16:13), bears witness to our new citizenship (Rom. 8:16), gives gifts (I Cor. 12:1), directs our path (Gal. 5:16), produces fruit (Gal. 5:22,23), fills (controls) (5:18), arms (6:17,18), exhorts (Rev. 2:7) and much, much more. Understanding the character and activity of the Holy Spirit is essential to maintaining the unity of the body!

One hope

The members of this <u>one body</u>, instructed and led by <u>one Spirit</u> also share a common hope. The content of this hope is ultimate and eternal redemption (Rom 8:23) and the fulfillment of all of God's promises. It is unseen (Rom. 8:24), based in our relationship with Christ (Col. 1:27), laid up (preserved) for us in heaven (Col. 1:5). Because of all that this hope enfolds we wait for it eagerly (Gal. 5:5) and it continues to be an incentive for faithful living and service (Titus 2:13, Heb. 6:11).

Paul's first prayer for the Ephesians (1:15-23) was that "they would know what is the hope to which he has called you" (1:18). He follows that immediately by calling attention to "the riches of his glorious inheritance in the saints" (1:18). Therefore I repeat my comment that having hope is living in the understanding that all God's promises will surely be fulfilled. Hope brings joy to our lives (Rom. 5:2, 12:12), encourages our witnessing (I Cor. 9:10, II Cor. 10:15, Titus 2:13, 3:4), and is an incentive for godly living (I John 3:3).

One LORD

Paul continues; there is "<u>one Lord</u>". This should be a no-brainer for every believer. The importance of this new entity, the Church, has been presented in this epistle and Christ has been placed by

God as <u>head of the Church</u> (1:22). That should be the end of any additional discussion. Jesus stated that even love of family must be subservient to our love of and submission to Him (Matt. 10:27). But, unfortunately, the Church (even the evangelical, orthodox) continues to allow other influences to curtail the Lordship of her Head. This is not usually done deliberately but when the focus on Christ becomes blurred, the expedient, the popular, the feel-good, the acceptable (by the majority) tend to show these not-so-beautiful faces. It takes some effort to keep our attention focused on the Head of the church but the result is great blessing.

In Paul's letters his first reference to Jesus is as the Lord Jesus Christ, or Jesus Christ our Lord, with the exception of his letter to Titus. We would also do well to become accustomed to referring to Him as "our Lord Jesus Christ". Remember, His is the Name above every name. If you have ever joined a choir singing Handel's *Messiah* you have had a foretaste of what it will be like when at the marriage supper of the Lamb we sing "Hallelujah! For the LORD our God the almighty reigns" (Rev. 19:6).

One Faith

And there is one faith. We often think of faith in two ways; as a body of truth and as a way of life. Jude appealed to his readers to "contend for the faith that was once for all delivered to the saints" (vs. 3). That seems to refer to a body of truth which the saints were to guard and submit to. Paul referred to "the church of the living God" as a "pillar and buttress of the truth" (I Tim. 3:15).

But faith is much more than a statement of doctrine. Faith is a way of life. The author of Hebrews gives us considerable light on living by faith. He wrote "without faith it is impossible to please him (God), for whoever would draw near to God must believe that he exists and that he rewards those who seek him" (Heb. 11:6). I think he is saying that true faith not only affirms the existence of God, but that belief in God makes a difference in how the believer lives. He then calls attention to a whole roster of those who lived like that. Convinced of the existence of a God who had revealed Himself made a significant difference in how they lived. Noah's faith saw him building an ark nowhere near any water. Abraham's faith caused him to leave the comfort of familiar ground and set out for nowhere. And the list goes on.

The question we now face is what influence does faith have in how we conduct our lives?

Living in faith is to be always aware of our relationship to God (Father, Son, Spirit). It is not becoming too comfortable here. It is like the elderly lady after her first airplane ride. I enjoyed the flight and felt I was safe but "I never did put my full weight down." That is how we need to live here, not putting our full weight down. I'm reminded of the song by Hank Thompson that our quartet used to sing.

> This world is not my home, I'm just a' passin through
> My treasures are laid up somewhere beyond the blue
> The angels beckon me from heaven's open door
> And I can't feel at home in this world anymore!

Living in, or by, faith is also "being prepared to make a defense to anyone who asks you for a reason for the hope that is in you" (I Pet. 3:15). Even, perhaps, to those who don't ask.

One Baptism

There is (only?) one Baptism. Seems a little odd, doesn't it, that this one baptism should be the cause of innumerable separations? Paul defines this one baptism in his letter to the Corinthians. He wrote "For in one Spirit we were all baptized into one body . . (I Cor. 12:13). Upon conversion we are placed into the body of Christ (1:23) by the Holy Spirit. And if there is just one baptism, then all the other mentions of baptism must be part of this one baptism Usually they are illustrations of, or remembrances, of the one Spiritual baptism. The Ethiopian eunuch was baptized as an affirmation of his faith and the work of God's Spirit in placing him into the body of believers. Even so our physical baptism, whatever form it might take, is an outward manifestation of what has taken place inwardly. It is an outward display of our inward identification with the Church, the body of Christ.

One God and Father

And all this is predicated on the over-riding truth that there is "one God and Father of all, who is over all and through all and in all" (4:6). To understand God as Father is the source of great comfort. Our prayers are addressed to Him as Father, the One who has our best interests always in mind. The unity of God the Father, God the Son (our one Lord), and God the Holy Spirit is the basis of our unity with the Trinity and with one another in the <u>one body.</u>

Equipping for Ministry in a Unified Body.

The Equipper

Possessing the essential qualities of humility, gentleness and patience, and assenting to the sevenfold unity of the body of Christ is a good start. But something more is needed for the body to grow to maturity. The needed equipment can be provided only by the head of the church. He acquired His authority by humbling Himself and "becoming obedient to the point of death" (Phil. 2:8). This necessitated his descending "into the lower parts of the earth" or, as some translate "the lower parts, the earth" (4:9). After that he ascended when God "raised him from the dead and seated him at his right hand in the heavenly places" (1:20). "And he put all things under his feet and gave him as head over all things to the church, which is his body, the fullness of him who fills all in all" (1:22,23).

To emphasize his point Paul inserts a quotation from Psalm 68. It is a picture of a victor in battle, returning triumphantly with a host of captives. "You ascended on high, leading a host of captives in your train and receiving gifts among men" (Psa. 68:18). At first glance it seems that Paul has misquoted this verse, changing the last phrase to "and he <u>gave</u> gifts to men" (4:8). I can only guess that as he contemplated Christ's position as head of the church he realized that he didn't need gifts from His followers to stroke His ego. His authority was not to receive, but to give gifts. What could He be given to make His joy in victory complete? We have nothing to offer the conquering hero apart from our praise and thankfulness. He is supremely qualified to equip His followers to work together to display His wisdom.

The Equipment

The equipment God provides for the building up of Christ's body, the Church, consists of men with specific God given abilities. They are the apostles, prophets, evangelists, pastors and teachers. In the Greek text they are all preceded by a definite article except teacher. The use of the definite article in Greek stresses the identity of an object. To get the sense of its use in English we might underline or capitalize the article and place extra stress on it when we read it. THE apostles, THE prophets, etc. These men involved in the founding of the early church were not ordinary individuals. They had extraordinary abilities, given by God's Spirit. They were fulfilling God's purpose, as introduced early in this letter, in preparing the Church to display God's manifold wisdom.

The word "teachers" is anarthrous, not preceded with an article. This has lead many to assume that it belongs to "pastor" and the two words should be read as pastor/teacher. This seems appropriate since teaching is a vital part of a pastor's ministry.

The gifted individuals are probably listed here in their order of importance. In I Cor. 12:28 Paul writes "And God has appointed in the church first apostles, second prophets, third teachers." Other gifts follow in no special order. Spiritual gifts are also listed in Paul's first letter to the Corinthians, chapter twelve.

The Apostles

The apostles were men who had had a personal relationship with Jesus. Paul, in authenticating his right as an apostle, wrote that Christ had appeared to His apostles after the resurrection and "last of all, as to one untimely born, he appeared also to me" (I Cor. 15:, 7, 8). The verb form of the word apostle is apostello. The word literally means "to send" so an apostle is a sent one. In the New Testament the word is used almost exclusively for a special group of men who had been with Jesus. Only twice in 81 appearances of this word does it refer to those not included in this group. In these two cases the translators wisely used "messenger" (II Cor. 8:23, Phil. 2:25).

When God's revelation was complete and the church was well grounded apostles were no longer necessary and the apostolate died with the apostles. However, the ministry associated with the apostles as "sent ones" has not come to an end. The early missionaries who introduced Christianity into new areas had ministries not unlike Paul's. And God continues to "send" laborers "to the end of the earth" (Acts 1:8).

The Prophets

He also gave the "prophets". The priests of the Old Testament represented the people before God. The prophets, on the other hand, represented God to the people. They were true prophets only if their message was from God and authenticated when their predictions came to pass (Deut. 18:22). Agabus, called a prophet in the New Testament also made predictions that came to pass (Acts. 11:27, 21:10-12). There were other prophets named in Acts including the daughters of Philip the Evangelist.

The word prophet is a combination of two words: pro, meaning for, and phemi, meaning to speak. A prophet, therefore, is one who "speaks for". In this context they are obviously those who speak for God. And there is no indication that they were limited to ministry in the early church. There are those today who have special abilities to proclaim God's truth. They may well be modern prophets. But we all have some ability, and some responsibility, to speak for God.

The Evangelists

God has also given to the church individuals who are gifted evangelists. They are able to articulate the Gospel clearly and secure fruitful responses. They were those who were burdened for the lost and founded missions and recruited workers to reach the lost. Paul's exhortation to Timothy could well be made to all of us, "Do the work of an evangelist" (II Tim. 4:5). Whether or not we have the gift of evangelism we have the responsibility, if not the rare privilege, of being faithful witnesses of His grace in our lives.

And He gave <u>the</u> pastors. This word for pastor is poine and it is translated in every other place as "shepherd". In speaking of His care for the sheep Jesus described Himself as the good shepherd. As the shepherd is responsible for the general needs of the flock, so the pastor is responsible for the needs of fellow believers. Perhaps the greatest need among God's new believers is teaching. Therefore we often refer to the shepherd as pastor/teacher.

These men were God's special gift to the church. The gifts they possessed we refer to as "leadership" gifts. They were fundamental to the establishing of the first churches and the abilities these gifts represented are essential to the church today. Their goal is "to equip the saints for the work of ministry, for building up the body of Christ" (4:12). As the saints use their gifts (see Romans 12 and I Corinthians 12) the church will be built up and "attain to the unity of the faith and the knowledge of the Son of God, to mature manhood" (maturity) (4:13).

Unity is achieved "when each part is working properly" (4:16). Paul emphasized to the Corinthians the importance of believers exercising their spiritual gifts "that there be no division in the body" (I Cor. 12:25). The body "builds itself up in love" (4:16), and is "held together by every joint" (4:16) when each part, every member, is contributing his God-given ability to the growth of the church. Too many believers are mere pew warmers and contribute nothing to the ministry of the church.

For the work of the ministry to be accomplished in the church by the harmonious activity of the saints, there must be a more than casual understanding of Scripture. After Paul had described the work of the Trinity in producing saints in Chapter one, he prayed that they, the saints, would have "a spirit of wisdom and revelation in the knowledge of him" (1:17). Peter's final exhortation to his readers was to "grow in the grace and knowledge of our Lord and Savior,

Jesus Christ" (II Per. 3:18). Centuries earlier, David had described the "blessed man" (saint?) as one whose "delight is in the law of the Lord, and on his law he meditates day and night" (Psa. 1:2). "The Law" in this Psalm encompasses all of God's revelation. And "meditation" is a careful contemplation of Scripture. Only then are we capable of "rightly handling the word of truth" (II Tim. 2:15). If we are unable to wield the "Sword of the Spirit, which is the word of God" we will be at the mercy of "the cosmic powers over this present darkness" (6:12).

CHAPTER 5

Ephesians 4:17-32

TRANSFORMATION

*"Do not be conformed to this world, but be
transformed by the renewal of your mind,
that by testing you may discern what is the
will of God, what is good and acceptable
And perfect." Romans 12:2*

Careful hindsight often brings foresight into sharper focus. In other words, we should learn from our mistakes. Paul reminds these Ephesians of what their life once was like to protect them from sliding back into it. At that time their understanding was darkened, (4:18) they were unable to think clearly (4:17), they had been callous (4:19), Greedy (4:19), Sensuous (4:19,22). These and other things they were to put off and he is about to present them with a list of things they were to put on.

A key concept in this section is change. Paul draws a sharp contrast between that which should characterize their lives now with what they had been. "If anyone is in Christ, he is a new creation. The old has passed away, the new has come" (II Cor. 5:17). In those days there was a sharp contrast between believers and non-believers. It seems that in our day the distinction has become blurred. It has become increasingly difficult to easily differentiate between the two. We might possibly have some difficulty convincing our neighbors that "one's life does not consist of the abundance of his possessions" (Luke 12:15).

Paul, following the example of Jesus, was fond of using every day illustrations in his teaching. He used athletes and soldiers to illustrate devotion to duty. In this letter and in other letters he used the functions of parts of the human body working together to illustrate the similar functions of members of the church. In this section he illustrates the change in the believers activity with the change of clothing. There were certain things they should take off and other things they needed to put on. The old is swapped for the new. We should never forget that we began our life in Christ with the "mother" of all swaps. We traded in our sin and guilt for His righteousness (II Cor. 5:21).

There are a number of changes that are necessary if we are "to be renewed in the spirit of your minds and to put on the new self . ." (4:23, 24). We must put off "lying" and "speak the truth" (4:25). In our modern culture lying is an acceptable way of life. Blaise Pascal, who lived in the 17th century, could have described our day when he wrote "truth is so obscured nowadays, and lies so well established that unless we love the truth we shall never recognize it". It has almost come to the point today that when someone speaks (especially politicians?) we assume they are lying until they are proven true. The days when "my word is my bond" have passed us by. The truth is compromised even in the church today. (More about truth when we get to chapter six.)

Paul continues, "be angry and do not sin." I do not think he is condoning anger but if we resolve quickly whatever caused it, it is not necessarily sinful. James exhorts believers to be "slow to anger" (James 1:19). Gustav Shaehlin, author of the definition of anger, the Greek orge, in the *Theological Dictionary of the New Testament* (65 pages) suggests that "if in James, one is to be slow to anger, in

Ephesians, one is to be quick to overcome it" (Vol. V, p. 421). If anger is harbored for any length of time it becomes sin. Therefore "do not let the sun go down on your anger" (4:26).

Opportunity is given to the devil when we succumb to his temptations, and this "grieves" the Holy Spirit. The Spirit shelters us from the devil's temptations and when we yield we intimate that He is unable to protect us. Does that really cause Him grief?

It's mind boggling to think that God has an emotional relationship with us. God asks, through the prophet Ezekiel, "Have I any pleasure in the death of the wicked" (Ezek. 18:23)? And the Psalmist writes "Great is the Lord, who delights (literally "finds pleasure) in the welfare of his servants" (Psalm 35:27). And "The Lord takes pleasure in those who fear him" (Psalm 147:11). "God so loved the world, that he gave his only Son" (John 3:16). John reminds us that God is Love, and that "we love because he first loved us" (I John 4:19. And Jesus' emotion is obvious when he cries "O Jerusalem, Jerusalem . . . How often would I have gathered your children together as a hen gathers her brood under her wings, and you would not" (Matt. 23:37)! I find it incredible that the triune God would have such an emotional relationship with His people. But then, we're family! To love Him with heart and soul and mind demands our complete commitment to him. How would you describe your commitment?

"Let the thief no longer steal." (4:28). This is so obvious that to mention it seems superfluous. Until we realize that stealing includes much more than just taking objects that belong to someone else - just as lying includes much more than not telling the truth. We can steal other's time when we are avoidably late for an appointment. Do we rob God of the honor due Him when we allow other things to divert our attention from Him? God spoke to Israel through the prophet Malachi, "You are robbing me" (Mal. 3:8). They had been withholding the tithes and offerings prescribed by the law.

Paul's exhortation to the Ephesians is put off stealing and put on working, "rather let him labor, doing honest work with his hands" (4:28) He then surprises us a little by listing the goal (or at least one goal) of honest labor, "so that he may have something to share with anyone in need" (4:28). I wonder how many of us consider this when we go to work. It is proper to work with the goal of providing for our family. But there should also be the desire to have something extra to share with those in need. And the need seems to be growing. There are millions, especially in Africa, who go to bed hungry every night. And the need for many to hear the Gospel does not diminish. It is shameful that the charitable giving of evangelicals to meet physical and spiritual needs is less than half of a tithe. We must do better than that. If you are serious about being faithful helpers in world evangelism I recommend a careful reading of II Corinthians, chapters eight and nine.

And put off "corrupting talk" and put on "such as is good for building up" (4:29). There is probably no part of our anatomy that gets us into more trouble than the tongue. You probably (unfortunately) have never heard of the exploits of the great Minnesota (other states have tried to adopt him) lumberjack, Paul Bunyan. Folklore informs us that the Grand Canyon was formed when he dragged his axe behind him. Among the many stories about him is the story of the Winter of the Blue Snows. It was so cold that winter that words that were spoken would immediately freeze. In the spring the words began to melt and people were mortified by the words they had spoken.

I am quite certain that we all have spoken words that we would like to recall. James had it right when he described the tongue as "a fire, a world of unrighteousness". It stains "the whole body, setting on fire the entire course of life" (James 3:6). It is in desperate need of being "tamed" so that it produces only words that are "good for building up . . . That it may give grace to those who hear" (4:29).

The things that he exhorts us to put off, "bitterness and wrath and anger and clamor and slander . . malice" (4:31) will disappear if we will "be kind to one another, tenderhearted, forgiving one another as God in Christ forgave you" (4:32). May I suggest that if we give diligence to "put on" these attributes, the "putting off" will be a great deal easier.

CHAPTER 6

Ephesians 5:1-16

OUR NEW WALK

*"We were buried therefore with him by baptism
into death, in order that, just as Christ was
raised from the dead by the glory of the
father, we too might walk in newness
Of life." Romans 6:4*

Jesus' life and ministry was all about displaying the wisdom of God. In writing about the foolishness of men in Chapter one of I Corinthians Paul presented Jesus Christ "whom God made our wisdom" and then added "and our righteousness and sanctification and redemption" (I Cor. 1:30). If we, then, are also to display God's wisdom, we must "therefore be imitators of God as beloved children." (5:1). Paul had exhorted the Corinthians to "be imitators of me as I am of Christ" (I Cor. 11:1). This was right after he had said that his desire was to "give no offense to Jews or to Greeks or to the church of God, just as I try to please everyone in everything I do, not seeking my own advantage, but that of many, that they may be saved" (I Cor. 10:33). We would do well to imitate Paul in these matters.

We saw in chapter one that we who believe were placed <u>in</u> Christ. If we are so intimately related to Him, then should we not share some of his genes? The things that characterized his life should also be among our qualities.

Walking in Love.

Paul reminded the Galatians that "the whole law is fulfilled in one word; you shall love your neighbor as yourself" (Gal. 5:14). You probably think "that is more than one word". But the word Paul uses is more than a collection of syllables. It is the word "logos" which is the word used to describe Jesus in John 1. "In the beginning was the word (logos)" (John 1:1). This word came to reveal God to mankind. A better translation than "word" in this context might be "concept". To love God with all our heart and soul and mind and to love our neighbor as ourselves is the fulfillment of the law (see Exodus 20). But we obviously need a little help in doing that.

And perhaps Dr. G. Campbell Morgan can help us. In a sermon on the fruit of the Spirit (Gal. 5:22,23) he reminds us that in the original text of the New Testament there was no punctuation. In fact there were no spaces between words. He suggests that after "the fruit of the Spirit is love" (note that the verb is singular) we place a semicolon and perhaps a dash and then continue "joy, peace," etc. He ends up defining "The fruit of the Spirit is love" as "If you have love you have all these things. Joy is its consciousness. Peace is its confidence. Long-suffering is its habit. Kindness is its activity, Goodness is its quality. Faithfulness is its quantity. Meekness is its tone. Self-control is its victory." (*The Westminster Pulpit,* Vol. 1, page 178) This is the love Paul exhorts the Ephesians, and us, to "walk in". This deserves some meditation.

If we are motivated by this love, sexual immorality is impossible. Coveting something, or someone, belonging to another is off the table. Filthy or foolish talk, crude joking or empty words are incompatible with love for God and our fellow humans. These activities that define the unbelievers have no place in the lives of those who "walk in love". The One we love, because He first loved us (I John 4:19) will lead us in the paths of righteousness (Psa. 23:3) because "your word is a lamp to my feet and a light to my path" (Psa. 119:105).

Walking in Light

There is nothing more conducive to walking in love than to allow God's light to consistently illumine our path. The Apostle John reminds us that not only is God love, but he is also light. "And if we walk in the light, as he is in the light, we have fellowship with one another, and the blood of Jesus his Son cleanses us from all sin" (I John 1:7).

As paratroopers in WWII we were privileged to wear boots that actually could be polished. We were proud of those boots and were diligent in bringing them to a high gloss. After I was discharged from the army my interest in shiny shoes waned. However, one day I spent some time putting (what I thought was) a high gloss on my shoes. When I finished I placed them in a spot where bright sunlight was streaming through the window. To my disappointment, the light revealed numerous flaws in my handiwork. I was reminded of John's words that "God is light and in him is no darkness at all" and "if we walk in the light as he is in the light . . The blood of Jesus his Son cleanses us from all sin" (1:7). Only as we walk in close fellowship with Him will His light illumine the many flaws in our lives so we will recognize and confess our sin to experience His forgiveness (I John 1:9).

Walk Carefully

The word translated "carefully" (akribos) in the ESV is found 5 times in the New Testament. We read in Matthew 2:8 that the wise men were instructed by Herod to search "diligently" - same word - for the child who was to be king of the Jews. Luke wrote that he had followed the events of the apostles "closely" (Luke 1:3) and also wrote that Apollos had taught "accurately" the things concerning Jesus (Acts 18:25). And Paul described the Thessalonians as being "fully aware" of the uncertainty of the Day of the Lord. The same Greek word is used in these 4 places and also in Ephesians 5:15.

From these uses of this word we get some idea of the gravity of its meaning. The AV has translated the word as "circumspectly" which Webster defines as "careful to consider all circumstances and possible consequences". Not a bad translation!

For Paul the christian's life was not a "walk in the park". If in our election and predestination God had a specific purpose for us then how we conduct our walk is of eternal importance. Art Linkletter wrote a book entitled *"Growing Old is not for Sissies."* Nor is walking with Jesus. Just ask believers in North Korea or in many Muslim dominated nations. A father, concerned about his son in college, asked "Son, does being a Christian make life difficult for you?" His response was, "No, Dad, they don't even know I'm a Christian." If our life is a bed of roses, with no speed bumps in the way, perhaps its because we are not pursuing God's purpose in us "carefully". We are much too nonchalant about our walk. God has obviously paid careful attention to the details of our life. Shouldn't we as well?!

A vital part of our "careful" walk is to be walking "not as unwise, but as wise" (5:15). Christianity is a "thinking" persons way of life. Jesus, preparing to send His disciples out as witnesses, instructed them to be "wise as serpents and innocent (the word usually translated as "harmless" in the NT) as doves" (Matt. 10:16). Paul paraphrased that quote from Jesus as "to be wise as to what is good and innocent (harmless) as to what is evil" (Rom. 16:19). A wise (?) man once said "a few people think, a few more think they think and the rest would rather die than think". The greatest activity our minds can be involved in is to think God's thoughts after Him. That requires a more than casual study of the revelation of Himself in Scripture. And "if any of you lacks wisdom, let him ask of God, who gives generously to all without reproach, and it will be given him" (James 1:5).

Walking "carefully" also means "making the best use of the time, because the days are evil" (5:16). We often complain that there aren't enough hours in the day. We will have to argue with God about that because he obviously determined that 24 were sufficient.

There actually was one time when 24 hours were not enough. Joshua, in a battle with the Amonites prayed for a few more hours to complete his victory. God evidently agreed that 24 hours that day were insufficient. And God graciously provided an additional 24 or perhaps 12 (whole day) (Joshua 10:12-14). That incident reveals to us that if we really needed extra time, God would provide it. Our problem is not that we have insufficient time, the problem is that we don't use it wisely.

The word Paul uses for "making the best use of" is the Greek exagarazo. Agarazo is usually translated "to buy" though it can also be translated "to redeem" as in "Christ has redeemed us from the curse of the law" (Gal. 3:13). The prefix "ex" or "ek" means out of. So Paul is encouraging us to "redeem" our time; to buy it "out of" the evil days. Which is to make the best use of it. I don't know if our days are more evil than Paul's days. I am quite certain they are more evil than they were a century ago, at least in our country. Which makes it all the more important to "redeem" it. To guard it "carefully" so it won't be lost in the malaise of the "evil days".

And we need to "understand what the will of the Lord is." We usually consider the will of the Lord as it relates to life choices. What kind of work should I consider, where should I live, who will be my life partner?, etc. The writers of Scripture, at least in my estimation, do not think of the will of God in those terms. I think the Scriptural view of the will of God is summed up by Paul when he wrote "For this is the will of God, your sanctification: that you abstain from sexual immorality: that each one of you know how to control his own body in holiness and honor . ." (I Thes. 4:3,4). It is God's will that we put off the works of the flesh and put on the fruit of the Spirit. If we display the breastplate of righteousness all the other life choices will sort themselves out. "But seek first the kingdom of God and his righteousness, and all these things will be added to you" (Math. 6:33).

CHAPTER 7

Eph. 5:18 - 6:9

BE FILLED WITH THE SPIRIT

*"And they were all filled with the Holy
Spirit and began to speak in other
tongues as the Spirit gave them
utterance." Acts 2:4*

Perhaps the most important contribution to walking "carefully" is to be "filled with the Spirit" (5:18). From a study of the use of the word "filling" in the New Testament and as it is defined by Kittel (*Theological Dictionary of the New Testament*), there is a sense of totality or completeness with this word. Paul states in his first prayer (1:23) that the church somehow "fulfills" or completes the Head of the church. In his second prayer he prays that these Ephesians would be "filled with all the fullness of God" (3:19). This fullness is a result of their being "strengthened with power through his Spirit" (3:16), "rooted and grounded in love" (3:17), "strengthened to comprehend with all the saints what is the breadth and length and height and depth" (3:18). That is certainly being "filled with all the fullness of God" and can only be achieved through the ministry of God's Spirit at work in the life of the believer.

We understand this concept of fullness even more clearly from the contrast Paul draws for us. He wrote "do not get drunk with wine but be filled with the Spirit" (5:18). Drunkenness is often defined as "being under the influence" of alcohol. We tend to forgive the drunkard for not being responsible. His actions are influenced by the alcohol in his physical body. Similarly, if our spiritual body (nature) is "filled" with God's Spirit our activities will be influenced by Him. "But I say, walk by the Spirit and you will not gratify the desires of the flesh" (Gal. 5:16). Jesus promised His disciples that after His ascension He would send them a "helper, the Holy Spirit, whom the Father will send in my name, he will teach you all things and bring to your remembrance all that I have said to you" (John 14:26). Armed by God's word and influenced and strengthened by His Spirit we are able to avoid the works of the flesh (Gal. 5:19-21) and display the fruit of the Spirit (5:22,23).

Being filled with the Spirit produces qualities that are evidences of His influence in us. They are joy, thankfulness and submission. There are other evidences as well but Paul spells out these three, especially the last, in some detail.

Joy

This Spirit filled joy is revealed in both our relationships with one another and our relationship with the triune God. We express our joy with one another "in psalms and hymns and spiritual songs" (5:19) We can interpret that both literally and figuratively. We do it by actually singing together. We all, I am quite certain, have very fond memories of singing together with our friends around a campfire or while traveling together to camp or other gatherings. In addition we experienced and displayed our joy in pleasant conversations, working together and just being together.

We express our joy in and to God "singing and making melody to the Lord with all your (our) heart" (6:19). I recently read the autobiography of a friend, who, with her husband, has served more than 50 years in various ministries in Europe and America. Joy and Bill Boerup, friends since the late 50's, have served sacrificially in many ministries, especially in spiritually dead Belgium. They often lived and worked under extremely difficult circumstances but the story of their lives and ministries is appropriately titled *Joy in Living*.(I suggest you read this book. You may find it at <u>www.pleasantwordbooks.com</u>)

Our joy in fellowship and in ministry is predicated on our joy in the Lord. David lost his joy when he allowed his flesh to dictate his desires. When he confessed, was forgiven and again allowed his Shepherd to fulfill his desires, his joy was restored and his fruitfulness returned. "Then I will teach transgressors your ways" (Psa. 51:13). David wrote. A little more display of joy by those of us who claim Christ as our Shepherd would probably enhance our fruitfulness as witnesses.

Happiness is dependant on circumstances. Joy depends on a relationship. It is present no matter what the circumstances of life might be. You can even "Count it all joy, my brothers, when you meet trials of various kinds" (Jas. 1:2). And Peter reminds us that as we contemplate Christ's unseen presence in our lives we "rejoice with joy that is inexpressible and filled with glory" (I Pet. 1:8).

Thankfulness

Thanksgiving is much more than a national holiday. The word "thanks" should roll off our tongues like water off a duck's back. Offerings for thanksgiving were part of the Levitical sacrifices (Lev. 7:12-15). They were evidently designed to achieve a response as the psalmist suggests "Let us come into his presence with thanksgiving" (Psa. 95:2). At the dedication of the rebuilt walls of Jerusalem, Nehemiah organized two great choirs for the express purpose of voicing their thanks to God for this achievement (Neh. 12:31, 38). This was evidently done in response to Nehemiah's understanding of Scripture, "For long ago in the days of David and Asaph there were directors of the singers, and there were songs of praise and thanksgiving to God" (Neh. 12:46). The prophet Jeremiah had written about the New Covenant and those who would be a part of it, "out of them shall come songs of thanksgiving" (Jer. 30:19).

Now living under the New Covenant we are encouraged, no, exhorted to express our continuing gratefulness for enjoying this covenant relationship. How often do we echo the words of Paul to the Corinthians, "Thanks to be God for his inexpressible gift" (II Cor. 9:15)! Paul wrote the Colossians that while being "built up" in Christ, they were to be "abounding in thanksgiving" (Col. 2:7). The Philippians were instructed to offer their prayers "with thanksgiving" (Phil. 4:6). In the final instructions in his first letter to the Thessalonians Paul urges them to "give thanks in all circumstances, for this is the will of God in Christ Jesus for you" (I Thes. 5:18). Do you get the feeling that thanksgiving should be a vital part of your life?

A very sad incident in Jesus' life is recorded by Luke. On one occasion Jesus had healed ten lepers. Of the ten, only one returned and "fell on his face at Jesus' feet, giving him thanks" (Luke 17:16). Thanklessness is characteristic of those who reject God's offer of Grace. "For although they knew God, they did not honor him as God or give thanks to him . ." (Rom. 1:21). Among the first words our parents taught us to say were "please" and "thanks". Thank you notes seem to have followed the dinosaurs into extinction.

Submission

To "be filled with the Spirit", Paul affirms, produces joy and thankfulness. It also produces a third quality that is more demanding. This is where, as J. Vernon McGee would say, "the rubber meets the road." In the following verses Paul will underline the importance of submission in several different relationships: husband/wife, parent/child, and master/slave. In all of these relationships submission is a response to various circumstances in various ways. How we respond should not depend on our relationship to the "respondee" but on our relationship to the Spirit who enables our ability to submit. We submit "to one another out of reverence for Christ" (5:21). Paul continues to remind us He is "the head over all things to the church" (1:23), and we are the church!

The word translated "submission" is the Greek "hupotassomai" which means to place under, or be placed under, someone or something. It can be voluntary or compulsory. In the case of Jesus, His submission to Mary and Joseph was obviously voluntary. As Paul presents submission here in Ephesians it may be seen as either voluntary or compulsory. It is voluntary in that it cannot be forced on anyone. On the other hand it may be viewed as compulsory since one cannot claim to be filled with the Spirit and refuse to be submissive.

The desire and ability to be submissive is a characteristic of the mature believer. Paul encouraged submission not only in the areas he presents here, but in every relationship of our lives. He encouraged submission in our relationship to our weaker brethren. "We who are strong have an obligation to bear with the failings of the weak, and not to please ourselves" (Rom. 15:1). We voluntarily give up certain freedoms so as "never to put a stumbling block or hindrance in the way of a brother (or sister)" (Rom. 14:13). This relates to being "eager (spoudazomai) to maintain the unity of the Spirit in the bond of peace" (4:3). Is this not compulsory if we claim to be filled (controlled) by the Spirit?

Submission in the husband/wife relationship.

Paul becomes very specific when he writes of the need of submission in several different relationships. The first one he deals with, the husband/wife relationship, is vitally important because it also is a picture of the relationship of the church to its head. And he states unequivocally, "Wives, submit to your own husbands, as to the Lord. For the husband is the head of the wife even as Christ is the head of the church . ." (5:22,23). The husband's authority is based, at least in part, on the fact that man was created first (I Tim. 2:13). His headship in the family is similar to Christ's headship to the church. The wife, therefore, should pattern her submission to her husband as the church is in submission to Christ.

This is obviously not an unimportant or easily achieved responsibility. But it is greatly mitigated by Paul's additional exhortation to husbands to "love your wives as Christ loved the church and gave himself up for her" (5:25). It would be very difficult to decide who has the most difficult responsibility. The responses of both are extremely important because they illustrate the relationship of Christ to His body, the church. Christ's care for His church is a pattern for the husband's care for his wife. As Christ has made provision for the health and other needs of the church so the husband must care for the health and other material needs of his wife. As Christ is concerned for the purity of His church, so must the husband as priest in his home, care for the spiritual needs of his wife. And as Christ assures the unbreakable relationship to His Body, so should the husband be concerned with the permanent relationship in his home.

Christ contributes to the growth of the body by equipping members of the body with differing gifts. The husband cannot equip his wife with gifts, but is it not his responsibility to help the wife discover her gifts and abilities in ministry to the family and in the church? A man is a fool if he does not listen to his wife, and in some cases submit to her insight in making important decisions.

The relationship initiated in the garden between one man and one woman is ignored at our peril. Its abuse has caused untold misery over the centuries - read the Old Testament. The current breakup of the edenic family structure has left lives strewn with debris. Families without fathers have been incubators of poverty and crime. We have paid an extremely high penalty for this particular sin. I wonder if a, if not the, besetting sin of women is to desire control. And perhaps that of men is to encourage them. It is hard to improve on a family with a submissive (read "respectful") mother and a loving (agape, not phileo) father.

Christ's activity on behalf of His church was "so that he might present the church to himself in splendor, without spot or wrinkle or any such thing, that she might be holy and without blemish" (5:27). It is obvious that husbands will never be able to live up to the standard set by our Lord Jesus Christ. But that should not discourage husbands from giving it their best shot. In the words of Robert Browning, "ah, but a man's reach should exceed his grasp, or what's a heaven for?" The blessedness obtained by this Scriptural relationship of one woman and one man is its own reward. But it has the additional blessing of being a picture of Christ's relationship to His church.

Submission in the child/parent relationship

To the respectful wife and the loving husband, add an obedient child, and you have a picture, the beauty of which no artist could paint. After the first four commandments which govern our relationship to God, the next one is to children. "Honor your father and your mother, that your days may be long in the land that the Lord your God is giving you" (Ex. 20:12). The Israelites took this commandment very seriously. The duplicate record of the Law in Deuteronomy demanded harsh treatment of stubborn and rebellious sons. After being given every opportunity to obey their parents and continuing to refuse they were to be stoned (Deut. 21:18-21). It's interesting that rebellious daughters are not mentioned. Perhaps daughters in those days were less prone to rebellion, or their obedience was less significant than that of sons and their future as fathers. Eli, the priest, was severely chastened by God, for his failure to exercise discipline with his sons. Among Paul's qualifications for elders in I Tim. 3 and Titus 1 he lists the ability to manage their households well. This would include control of his children. In Titus he adds his children must be believers. It seems to me that that could be interpreted as "faithful" children, which would describe them as being managed well.

To the 5th commandment, recorded in Exodus 20 and repeated in Deuteronomy 5, Paul adds an exhortation to fathers. "Fathers, do not provoke your children to anger, but bring them up in the discipline and instruction of the Lord" (6:4). He appears to be claiming that the father has the ultimate responsibility for the discipline and training of his children. He will, obviously, designate considerable responsibility to the mother since she will spend considerably more time with the children.

No Scripture verse has been quoted more often when considering child training than Proverbs 22:6. "Train up a child in the way he should go; even when he is old he will not depart from it." Like all proverbs, this statement is generally true, but probably not without exceptions. If there were no exceptions to this statement it would place an unbearable burden on parents. But the fact that it is usually true does place a responsibility on the parents to be diligent in the training and discipline of children. The phrase "in the way he should go" might also be read as "in his own way." *The Bible Knowledge Commentary* interprets this as "according to demands of personality, conduct or stage of life". If you have more than one child you already realize that each child is different. "One size fits all" certainly doesn't apply. It is necessary to give diligence to understanding our children and suiting our discipline and instruction to their needs and dispositions.

In Paul's rather limited instruction to parents he adds, "fathers, do not provoke your children to anger". I suppose fathers are more prone to do this than are mothers. Perhaps the greatest provocation to anger stems from parental inconsistencies. When a parent gives in to children's desires repeatedly and suddenly decides to clamp down the children's anger is understandable. Better to be consistent so the children know what to expect. Dr. James Dobson states that we program our children. We teach them to respond only when "I really mean it" emerges at about the 3rd and 4th request for obedience. If we were to demand response the first time that would contribute to the child's well-being, as well as to a great deal more tranquility in the home. If we were to demand (encourage?) submission in the home perhaps submission to Jesus Christ might come more easily when the children leave home.

As we consider the importance of training children we need to be reminded that children are not exempt from our mission of "making disciples" by evangelizing and teaching. Too many of our offspring leave home with King James vocabulary but no personal relationship with the Lord Jesus Christ. Don't allow that to happen in your home.

The Master/Slave Relationship 6:5-9.

Paul opens this section with "Slaves, obey your earthly masters with a sincere heart . ." (6:5). There were obviously slaves in the churches and Paul does not discourage them from seeking freedom (I Cor. 7:21). But those who continue as slaves Paul exhorts to render faithful service to their masters. This service is to be extended "as to the Lord", which will make their service much more satisfying.

If there were slaves in the churches there were probably also masters, and Paul also has instruction for them. He reminds them that they, as well as their slaves, have a "Master" in heaven who harbors no partiality. Therefore they must treat their slaves "justly and fairly" (Col. 4:1). Unfortunately (from our point of view) Paul does not elaborate on those adverbs, but if these masters have been following his prior words they would know exactly how to treat their slaves.

In our Christian culture there are no longer masters and slaves. But the principles Paul has espoused can be transferred directly into the modern employer/employee relationship. An employee is responsible to render faithful service to his employer. He is to do "honest work with his own hands" (4:28) and that will be easier and more fulfilling if among his goals is to "have something to share with anyone in need" (4:28). An employee is to supply a full day's work for the employer's responsibility to provide a fair day's pay.

The author of Hebrews introduces us to another relationship where submission is called for. "Obey your leaders and submit to them, for they are keeping watch over your souls, as those who have to give an account" (Heb. 13:17). Having served as an elder for many years I can testify that this is something that is not taken seriously by very many church members. I can list at least a dozen individuals (probably many times that number) who glibly professed submission when joining a church but whose submission evaporated when their desires were not achieved. A submissive life style is the product of walking in humility, gentleness and patience; giving faithful diligence to maintaining the unity of the Spirit; and who share with fellow believers partnership in one body; lead by one Spirit; sharing the one hope; submissive to one Lord; subscribing to one faith; baptized by one Spirit into the one body; convinced there is one God and Father of all who is over all and through all and in all. (4:1-6) That's more than a mouthful and demands some thoughtful meditation.

CHAPTER 8

Ephesians 6:10-24

ARMED FOR CONFLICT

> *"Have I not commanded you? Be strong*
> *and courageous. Do not be frightened,*
> *and do not be dismayed, for the Lord*
> *your God is with you wherever*
> *you go." Joshua 1:9*

ARMED FOR CONFLICT

Paul opens this final section of his letter with the word(s) "finally" (tou loipou). The primary meaning of the word is "the rest" or "remaining". It is also translated as "henceforth" (II Time 4:8), "from now on" (I Cor. 7:29) "moreover" (I Cor. 4:2). The word seems to relate what follows to what has gone before. And what follows this word in this context is in some sense a recap of what has been presented up to this point. He has taken the concepts of truth, righteousness, gospel, faith, salvation and Scripture and reinterpreted them in a way that makes them relatively easy to apply.

When he encouraged his readers to "be strong" he may very well have been thinking of God's challenge to Joshua as he is about to lead Israel into a new experience. This is not unlike the experience of the Ephesians as they are involved in the unfolding of a new phase in God's dealing with the human race. In praying that they would "be strengthened with power through his Spirit" (3:16) he has reminded them that their strength is dependant on "his might" (6:10).

Paul began this epistle by affirming that God's blessings are available "in the heavenlies". He again refers to "the heavenlies" in 2:6 as the place to which believers have been raised with Christ Jesus. In the first five chapters he has prepared his readers to discover that "in the heavenlies" is not only a place of blessing, but an arena of conflict also. And we should be grateful that this is true and that we can be involved. Without challenges life would be boring and the Christian's life should never be boring. We who live in the comforts of America should probably be praying with Isaac Watts

> Must I be carried to the skies
> On flowry beds of ease
> While others fought to win the prize,
> And sailed through bloody seas?

And after praying with Mr. Watts we should take up the challenge of Charles Wesley:

> Soldiers of Christ arise and put your armor on
> Strong in the strength which God supplies
> through his eternal son.
> to keep your armor bright attend with constant care
> still walking in your Captain's sight and watching unto
> prayer.

And the forces of evil "in the heavenlies" are nothing to be sneezed at. Paul almost seems to be exaggerating when he lists our enemies as "rulers", "authorities", "cosmic powers over this present darkness". All under the leadership of our adversary, the Devil. Someone is reported to having said "I don't believe there is a devil. I have never met him". The response was "two people traveling in the same direction rarely meet." If we are moving in the opposite direction we will surely meet him. Peter reminds us that "your adversary, the devil, prowls around like a roaring lion seeking whom he may devour" (I Pet. 5:8). Perhaps he is even more dangerous when he "disguises himself as an angel of light" (II Cor. 11:14). But fortunately "we are not ignorant of his designs" (II Cor. 4:11). Our struggle is not against physical forces, "for we wrestle not against flesh and blood" (6:12). Therefore, physical weapons are of no use in this conflict. Peter's sword was able to cut off the ear of the servant of the high priest, but it had no effect on the battle that was taking place.

The armor Paul describes is essential to "be able to withstand in the evil day" (6:13). He has already exhorted his readers to redeem "the time because the days are evil" (5:16). Jesus described those living in His day as an "evil and adulterous generation" (Matt 12:39). Is our generation more evil than was Paul's? He did inform Timothy that "evil people and imposters will go on from bad to worse" (II Tim. 3:13). The evil of our day is certainly no less evil than it was in Paul's day. Judge Robert Bork captured the spirit of this present age in his book, *Slouching toward Gomorah: Modern Liberalism and Moral Decline.* The culture of our age has certainly deteriorated in the last century, and deteriorated exponentially since the 1960's. The radicals of the 60's now control our universities and the entertainment and music industries; those elements of society that shape our culture.

While all our country's founding fathers were probably not true believers, they were friendly toward Scripture and Christians and our founding principles were unquestionably based on the Bible. In the last century that friendliness has turned to indifference and in the past decade this indifference has turned to open hostility. There have always been vocal atheists around like Ayn Rand and Madeline O'Hare. But recently several books by atheists have become bestsellers. *The Weekly Standard,* which is not a Christian publication, in an article entitled "What hath God Wrought" called attention to several of these: *The God Delusion,* by Richard Dawkins, a respected scientist, *The End of Faith,* by Sam Harris, *God is not Good,* by Christopher Hitchens, *Breaking the Spell,* by Daniel Dennett, and *Atheist Manifesto* by Michel Onfray. Christians are viewed by many as being as dangerous as radical Muslims and therefore must be marginalized.

In light of the rapid deterioration of our Christian culture Paul's exhortation to "take up the whole armor of God" is perhaps more essential for us today than it was in Paul's day. Paul was fond of using the illustration of "putting off" and "putting on" and used it in several of his epistles. He reminded the Galatians that "as many of you as were baptized into Christ have put on Christ" (Gal. 3:27). To the Romans he wrote "But put on the Lord Jesus Christ . ." (Rom. 13:14). He is now describing to the Ephesians what "putting on" the Lord Jesus Christ is all about. After informing the Ephesians, and us, what we are up against, he lists the items of body armor that assure victory over our invisible enemy.

The Belt of Truth

Paul begins by urging believers to "stand therefore, having fastened on the belt of truth" (6:14a). I don't believe there is any particular significance in the order in which Paul introduces the pieces of armor. But it is hardly possible to exaggerate the importance of truth. Wearing the belt of truth ought to set us apart from those who are at ease in this pagan culture. We have entered into an intimate relationship with the One who described Himself as "the way, the TRUTH, and the life" (John 14:6). Poet James Russell Lowell observed a century and a half ago that "truth is forever on the scaffold and error forever on the throne". And two centuries earlier mathematician and philosopher Blaise Pascal wrote "truth is so obscured nowadays and lies so well established that unless we love the truth we shall never recognize it." Can you imagine the shock these men would suffer if they were to suddenly emerge into our post-modern culture?

Objective truth has become a victim of modern thought. According to contemporary standards each person must now define truth for himself. What is true for you may not be true for me. And with the disappearance of truth there is no longer a basis for morality. A student, interviewed by Notre Dame sociologist Christian Smith, summed up most modern students view of morality. "I mean, I guess what makes something right is how I feel about it. But different people feel different ways, so I couldn't speak on behalf of anyone else as to what is right and wrong" (quoted by Columnist Dennis Prager, in *The Washington Times,* weekly edition, 9/26/11). In this age of nebulous truth, it seems to me to be the epitome of hypocrisy for Congress to convict anyone for lying (Scooter Libby). Honesty is so rare that when a child returns something to its rightful owner he is hailed as a hero.

In this culture of disregard for truth the Christian should stand out like a sore thumb. And many are. And in many countries this is costing them their lives. And truth is much more than relaying facts. Truth is a way of life! Ephesians 4:15 in most translations reads, "speaking the truth in love". But the verb "speaking" is not in the text. Literally it reads "truthing in love". Speaking the truth is only a part of living the truth. Being silent my sometimes be the equivalent of lying. We older folks remember Andy Griffith's convenient failure to inform a prospective buyer of his house of a few of the warts. But Opie, having just received a lecture on honesty, filled in the blanks. Sometimes our silence may loosen the belt of truth a tad.

As believers, the belt of truth must be tightly fastened around our waist. That means, in my perhaps jaundiced estimation, we have no secrets. Our lives should be an open book! Would our television viewing be the same if the elders were watching with us? Or would our response to thoughtless drivers be altered if we were accompanied by the deacons? It is no less than amazing that we could be more concerned about their view of us than of God's view. We should probably repeat the song we sang as children, "Be careful little hands what you do . . . There's a Father up above who is looking down in love, so be careful little hands (or eyes, or feet, or tongue) what you do."

I don't quite understand why Paul uses the figure of truth as a belt, or why it is presented as the first piece of armor to put on. Perhaps he mentioned this first because the belt is what holds everything together. It keeps your shirt (or breastplate of righteousness) tucked in, holds up your pants and it comes in handy to keep your sword at the ready. It therefore seems quite appropriate that in listing the Christian's armor he begins with the belt of truth.

The Breastplate of Righteousness

The next piece of armor Paul presents is the breastplate of righteousness. There are two kinds of "righteousness" mentioned in Scripture. There is <u>imputed</u> righteousness and <u>practical, or lived out</u> righteousness. Paul can't be talking about imputed righteousness because he asks us to "put it on". Imputed righteousness is already ours by virtue of our being "in Christ". We don't need to "put it on". Paul has stated clearly to the Corinthians that "He hath made him who knew no sin to be sin for us, that we might become the <u>righteousness</u> of God in him" (II Cor. 5:21).

The righteousness that Paul presents here is that which we are to exhibit because Christ's righteousness has been imputed to us. Paul has given us an indication of what that looks like in Chapter 4, verses 25-32. The breastplate wearer is scrupulously honest in all his relationships (4:25). He gives no opportunity to the devil by losing control of his emotions (4:26). His assets are the result of his own labor which he is willing to share with those in need (4:28). His speech is limited to only what edifies his listeners (4:29). His life is lived in submission to the Spirit who gave him life. Verses 31 and 32 encapsulate those virtues that burnish the breastplate and help to display God's wisdom. "Let all bitterness and wrath and anger and clamor and slander be put away from you, along with all malice. Be kind to one another, tenderhearted, forgiving one another as God in Christ forgave you."

In our materialistic culture, the use of the fruit of our labor (4:28) perhaps needs some special attention. This brings up the important question of Christian stewardship, which is obviously an important part of the breastplate. Paul dealt with this in some detail in his letter to the Corinthians ((II Cor. 8,9). In it he lays out some principles which should inform our charitable responsibilities.

The Macedonians were lauded by Paul because they had given according to their means "and beyond". Paul encouraged Timothy to instruct the rich (which by world standards would be all of us) "to be generous and ready to share" (I Time 6:18). He also instructed the Corinthians to give according to what they have. Faith Promise giving encourages us to prayerfully consider an amount that stretches our faith and then trust God to help us to meet that promise. There is obviously benefit in this and it certainly has resulted in increased giving to missions. However, I think it is even more important to be faithful stewards of what we have. Giving should be an important part of the Christians' budget. I heartily agree with the person who observed that you can tell a great deal more about a person's commitment to Christ by reading his check book than his diary. "You may give without loving, but you cannot love without giving." (Author unknown).

He further implores to give with fairness or equality. Still writing to the Corinthians," I do not mean that others should be eased and you burdened, but that as a matter of <u>fairness</u> your abundance at the present time should supply their need" (II Cor. 8:14). There are millions in our world who through no fault of their own live in abject poverty. Do we have any responsibility to help them? In addition to those involved in evangelism should we not be supporting organizations like Samaritans Purse, World Vision, The Salvation Army, etc. who are ministering to material as well as spiritual needs? I am not convinced that we make any real sacrifices in meeting physical and spiritual needs in out fallen world.

Paul informed the Corinthians that God loves a <u>cheerful</u> giver (II Cor. 9:7). And the word he uses is *hilaros,* the Greek equivalent of hilarious. Someone has exhorted believers to give til it hurts. I would suggest that you continue giving until it stops hurting. When we give as an investment in building the kingdom of God, giving becomes a joyful activity. An English Vicar was attempting to comfort a dying parishioner. This man was wealthy and his response was "It's all right for you to be happy, vicar, for you are sending your wealth ahead.

I'm leaving mine behind." Should we not pay as much attention to our spiritual portfolio as our financial one?

I recently read some statistics on charitable giving. The giving among evangelicals seems to be somewhere between 3 and 4 percent. I find that shameful! We often speak of "tithes and offerings" which in most cases is probably an exaggeration since a tithe is ten percent. In Paul's list of spiritual gifts in Romans 12 he identifies "contributing" as one of them. I have never met anyone who claimed to have that gift although I have heard of a few very wealthy individuals who give very generously (although there seems to be little sacrifice involved). Teachers are known to have the gift of teaching by exercising that gift. Evangelists are known to have the gift of evangelism by the fruitfulness of their witness. Perhaps we need to determine if we have the gift of contributing by additional contributing. It would be a pity to lose the joy and satisfaction of exercising that gift if we actually possessed it!

Gospel Shoes

Having fastened on the belt of truth and having polished our breastplate of righteousness, now front and center, visible to all, we are ready to consider Paul's teaching concerning the gospel. These Ephesians were certainly aware of Paul's definition of the gospel recorded in I Cor. 15:3,4 "that Christ died for our sins in accordance with the Scriptures, that he was buried, that he was raised on the third day in accordance with the Scriptures" His burial attested to the reality of His death, and that He was seen by Cephas and many others attested to the reality of His resurrection. Paul stated that he himself was "set apart for the gospel of God" (Rom. 1:1). Following that, the remainder of his life was focused on the gospel. Everything he did and everywhere he went was influenced by his view of the gospel and his commitment to proclaim the message he presented in Chapter 2. And referring to the gospel as "shoes for your feet" calls our attention to the responsibility we have as faithful witnesses to the

Gospel. Isaiah was exhorted to "go" with the message of repentance (Isa. 6:9). Jesus request to the church is to "Go therefore and make disciples . ." (Matt. 28:19).

Paul further affirmed that there is a "readiness" attached to the gospel of peace. Paul sensed this "readiness" and was "eager to preach the gospel to you also who are in Rome." (Rom. 1:15). Peter agreed with Paul and exhorted his readers that they should always be prepared "to make a defense to anyone who asks you for a reason for the hope that is in you" (I Pet. 3:15).

The verb form of the word translated "readiness" (hetoimasia) is usually translated "to prepare", as in John 14 where Jesus informs His disciples "I go to prepare a place for you" (vs. 2). According to Walter Grundman in his definition of this word in the *Theological Dictionary of the New Testament*, the translators of the Old Testament into Greek considered this word "as suitable for expressing God's whole creative action in every age and at every moment in nature and history" (Vol. II, p.705,706). In commenting on this passage in Ephesians he added "This readiness gives the Christian life a distinctive dynamic character." This should characterize our relationship to the gospel. Putting on the Christian's armor should thoroughly prepare us to be faithful witnesses of the regenerative power of the gospel. And it should remind us that the gospel is thoroughly prepared to transform lives for it is "the power of God for salvation to everyone who believes" (Rom. 1:16).

In view of the power of the gospel and our preparation as witnesses how can we be content to let our "gospel shoes" sit unused in the closet? If the primary purpose of the church is to "display the manifold wisdom of God" (3:10) it should be our desire to make his wisdom known to as many people as possible. Every believer ought to have some evangelistic goal. Perhaps we should set up some tangible targets to whom we will witness - individuals for whose salvation we will pray passionately and persistently.

How intimately are we involved in the mission program of our church? Paul, recounting his suffering in preaching the gospel, wrote to the Corinthians "You also must help us by prayer so that many will give thanks on our behalf for the blessings granted us through the prayers of many" (II Cor. 1:11). This verse has already appeared several times in this commentary because of its importance in our display of the wisdom of God. How we view our responsibility to the gospel must have a significant influence in our lives. Does it make a difference in how we spend out time and our money? It should!

The Shield of Faith

Not only is the shield of faith essential in protecting us from the evil one, but "without faith it is impossible to please him" (God). The author of Hebrews continues, "for whoever would draw near to God must believe that he exists and that he is a rewarder of those who seek him" (Heb. 11:6). True faith is having an adequate understanding of the living God, and that understanding must make a difference in our lives. The author of Hebrews (whoever he might be) then presents an impressive list of those who exercised that kind of faith. One day faith will be sight, but until that day we live by faith. There is probably no concise definition of faith that is adequate. But to sum up, faith is placing our trust in God, placing ourselves at His disposal, and being content in whatever experience He is putting us through. That kind of faith is adequate protection against the darts of the evil one.

We all, I think, are targets of the dart of pride. This dart is deflected when faith kicks in and with James and Peter remember that exaltation follows humility (Jas. 4:10, I Pet. 5:6). The dart of doubt is dispelled when we repeat with Paul, "I know whom I have believed . ." (II Tim. 1`:12). The arrow of worldly desire falls short when we realize that by walking in the Spirit we lose interest in gratifying these desires (Gal. 5:16). The darts of jealousy and strife disappear when we consider others more significant than ourselves (Phil. 2:3). They may actually not be but that is beside the point. These are just a small sample of the many arrows Satan has in his quiver. But whatever ones may be aimed at us, our faith in God's revelation will be the means to quench every dart.

The Helmet of Salvation

The head is the most vulnerable part of our body. Remembering one of the old Burma Shave signs seems appropriate here, "Don't lose your head to save a minute, you need your head, your brains are in it!" And the special protection provided for the head and its contents is "Salvation". The concept of salvation encompasses all other concepts of Scripture. Included are justification, sanctification, glorification, and every other concept of theology. This knowledge is our ultimate protection. Our past, present, and future are all included. When we say we are saved, we've said it all.

The Sword of the Spirit

Some have considered the first five pieces of armor defensive and only the last one an item for offense. I don't think you can make that distinction. Standing firm for the truth is a powerful offensive weapon. Living righteously is a potent example that significantly enhances our ability to influence those to whom we witness. The gospel is a powerful defense against the wiles of Satan and a potent weapon in our hands when we witness to unbelievers. It then becomes the power of God for salvation. Faith is a part of our life from which no other part can be separate. And the "Sword of the Spirit which is the Word of God" is an all around weapon. It has incredible power since it is "living and active, sharper than any two-edged sword, piercing to the division of soul and spirit, of joints and of marrow, and discerning the thoughts and intensions of the heart" (Heb. 4:12). It is also a great defensive weapon. David wrote "I have stored up your word in my heart, that I might not sin against you" (Psa. 119:11).

It would be nice if all of these items were hanging on hooks in your closet, easily available to slip on when you arose in the morning. It isn't quite that easy, but it need not be all that hard either. When you put on your belt determine that your actions that day will be characterized by truthfulness and transparency. As you button your shirt or blouse ask God to help you to display His righteousness in a world where sinfulness is the norm. As you slip into your shoes prepare yourself to give an account of your faith and be ready to be a witness to the Gospel as you have opportunity. Always remembering that we are to walk by faith and not by sight, being assured that our past, present and future are all taken care of. And finally, as you place your wallet in your purse or pocket (reminded of the power of the almighty dollar) remember that we have the Word of God, the ultimate weapon in our battle against the forces of darkness and indifference.

Just a few years after sending this letter to the believers in Ephesus, Paul sent another letter to Ephesus. This letter was addressed to Timothy, who was probably ministering to the church at this time. It contained detailed instructions on how to fulfill his pastoral responsibilities. Inserted in this instructional manual for pastors was an important statement that seems appropriate to consider in our meditation on the armor of God. "Now there is great gain in godliness with contentment" (I Tim. 6:6).

Paul, in essence, was describing the one who has taken up "the whole armor of God". Godliness is displaying the wisdom of God, and putting on the whole armor will surely produce contentment. Each piece of armor contributes something special to the believer's contentment. The belt of truth, among other things, is a reminder of Jesus' words to His Disciples "you will know the truth, and the truth will set you free" (John 8:32). The chains of ignorance that cause uneasiness are broken as we fix our minds on the One who is "The Truth".

Wearing the Breastplate of Righteousness is displaying the wisdom of God and emphasizes our contentment in a world characterized by discontent. Fitted with "Gospel shoes" we are content that as Ambassadors for Christ we will see lives transformed by the Gospel. The Shield of Faith is a constant reminder that we are neither saved nor sanctified by our works. Our confidence is not in ourselves, but in the One whose death secured our salvation and shields us from the enemy's onslaughts. The Helmet of Salvation, protecting the most vulnerable part of our (spiritual) anatomy, provides the assurance that we "are saved to the uttermost" (Heb. 7:25). And armed with the Sword of the Spirit, infinitely more powerful than Excalibur, we have adequate defense against the wiles of the devil and our own fleshy desires. Additionally, it is a potent weapon of offense as we faithfully bear witness to the Gospel.

We have no reason not to sleep well tonight! Or do we?

The Quintessential Component

Paul now takes up the importance of prayer but not as the seventh piece of armor; because prayer is an essential ingredient of every piece of armor. Nothing operates properly unless it's watered with prayer. Truth is available only from God and is ours for the asking. The qualities displayed by the breastplate of righteousness would be impossible to produce apart from our prayerful dependence on the filling of God's Spirit. The fruitfulness of our witness of the gospel is totally dependent on the work of God's Spirit which is also influenced by our prayers. And we pray with the father of the boy with the unclean spirit recorded in Mark 9, "I believe; help my unbelief". The assurance that we are safely hidden in the helmet of salvation is ours through prayer. And the sword of the Spirit would be impotent unless its use is accompanied by earnest prayer.

Paul's additional statements about the importance of prayer should probably cause us to take stock of the content of our prayers. As he dictated this letter he was sitting in prison. His food was probably meager and judging from his later request to Timothy (II Tim. 4:13) his room was probably unheated. And what was his request? Pray "also for me that words may be given me in opening my mouth boldly to proclaim the mystery of the gospel . ." (6:19). Paul was the ultimate missionary. His overriding concern was not for himself but for those who were "alienated from the commonwealth of Israel and strangers to the covenant of promise, having no hope and without God in the world" (2:12). He also urged them to "keep alert with all perseverance, making supplication for all the saints" (6:18). There are countless saints in many parts of the world who, like Paul, are suffering intense persecution for the sake of the gospel. Contact the organization Open Doors for information about these sufferers and how we can pray for them.

Personal

If this letter was a circular letter intended to be read in several different churches, then the final verses may well have been a note added especially to the church at Ephesus. Paul had spent considerable time in Ephesus and had probably established close personal ties to this church. The believers there must have had an emotional concern for Paul and his circumstances and Paul wanted to assure them that he was alright. Therefore he sent his beloved brother, tychicus, to be a source of encouragement to them. Tychicus was a little like a missionary returning home to report on his ministry. Just as we ought to wait with great anticipation the reports of our returning missionaries. The more we know about their work, the better prepared we are to help them by our prayers.

The last two verses expressed Paul's desire for the church at Ephesus, all the other churches of Asia Minor, and perhaps, as he looked into the future, all the churches from his day to ours. The words speak for themselves and what a fitting finale to this letter, and to my commentary. "Peace be to the brothers, and love with faith, from God the Father and the Lord Jesus Christ. Grace be with all who love our Lord Jesus Christ with love incorruptible."

THE END

Epilogue

Just about a generation after Paul had sent this letter to the church in Ephesus, another letter was addressed to the same church. This letter had been dictated to the Apostle John, who was in prison on the island of Patmos because of his faithful witness. His description of the one who dictated this letter is startling (see Rev. 1:12-16).

From the information included in this second letter, it seems the Belt of Truth was still firmly in place. The church had not yet succumbed to evil and had rejected the error of the Nicolaitans. The believers were lauded for their "works" and "toil" which intimates that their feet were still shod with "the gospel of peace". The Shield of Faith was still in use, as was the Sword of the Spirit. Their patient endurance indicated that the Helmet of Salvation had not been removed.

But (if we could only remove that little word from our vocabulary) there seems to have been some slippage in the Breastplate of Righteousness. In Paul's letter he had urged them to speak the truth in love (4:15) and to "walk in love" (5:1). Some thirty years later they had "abandoned the love you had at first" (Rev. 2:4). The love that characterized their initial response to the Gospel has faded. Normally, to achieve five out of six possibilities is quite good. But in our walk as believers it is unacceptable. To display God's wisdom properly, we must "take up the <u>whole</u> armor of God" (6:13). The failure of these Ephesians put them in great danger of losing their "lampstand" (Rev. 2:5). The lampstand was perhaps an illustration of the presence of God's Spirit.

Therefore, the message "of him who holds the seven stars in his right hand, who walks among the golden lampstands" (Rev. 2:10), was, "repent, and do the works you did at first" (Rev. 2:5). How could they not respond to such an appeal? We, of course, despite our great curiosity, have no way of knowing what their response was.

The church today is faced with similar temptations and a similar appeal. During twenty years as a Postal Inspector, my job performance in relation to my job description was formally evaluated annually. Actually, evaluation was constant since every activity, every investigation, every report was reviewed by someone. A proper self evaluation avoided the unhappy consequence of receiving a negative evaluation (and loss of financial reward). Should that not also be the experience of each member of the Body of Christ? The evaluation grid Paul presented to the Ephesians is equally valid for us. Is our walk characterized by humility, gentleness and patience? Do we make every effort (spoudazo - remember?) "to maintain the unity of the Spirit in the bond of peace" (4:3)? Are we contributing to the growth of the body by properly exercising our spiritual gift(s)? Is our walk characterized by the joy, thankfulness and submission that demonstrate that the Spirit actually controls our life? Finally, have we taken up the whole armor of God?

If you have responded to all the above with the affirmative you have probably wasted your time reading this commentary. If not, the appeal to us of the One who holds the seven stars in His hand, is identical. Repent!! And in our response what comfort do we receive from John. "If we confess our sins, he is faithful and just to forgive us our sins and to cleanse us from all unrighteousness" (I John 1:9).

The Christian life, as you no doubt have already experienced, is not a leisurely walk in the park. It demands concentrated effort. We need to exercise our spiritual muscles and enjoy the spiritual exhilaration of being faithful, which is like God's "well done" (not unlike the exhilaration I feel after a brisk half-hour swim). I became a believer in Jesus Christ in my teens and the path to maturity has been much too slow. Had I been exposed to these truths much earlier, I think my growth might have been accelerated.

If David's affirmation that even "the wrath of men shall praise you (God)" (Psa. 76:10), perhaps God can use my meditations to help someone. Your comments addressed to desau@cox.net would be welcomed.